Absolutely
A-Line

Absolutely A-Line

1 Easy Pattern = 26 Adorable Dresses for Girls

Wendi Gratz

LARK BOOKS

A Division of Sterling Publishing Co., Inc.

New York / London

Senior Editor
Valerie Van Arsdale Shrader

Editor
Nathalie Mornu

Art Director
Megan Kirby

Illustrator
Susan McBride

Art Production
Carol Morse

Photographer
Steve Mann

Cover Designer
Chris Bryant

Library of Congress Cataloging-in-Publication Data

Gratz, Wendi.
    Absolutely A-line : 1 easy pattern = 26 adorable dresses for girls / Wendi Gratz. -- 1st ed.
        p. cm.
    Includes index.
    ISBN 978-1-60059-377-2 (pb-pbk. : alk. paper)
    1. Girls' clothing. 2. Dressmaking--Patterns. I. Title.
    TT562.G67 2009
    646.4'3206--dc22

                                    2008054380

10 9 8 7 6 5 4 3 2 1

First Edition

Published by Lark Books, A Division of
Sterling Publishing Co., Inc.
387 Park Avenue South, New York, NY 10016

Text © 2009, Wendi Gratz
Photography © 2009, Lark Books, a Division of Sterling Publishing Co., Inc., unless otherwise specified
Illustrations © 2009, Lark Books, a Division of Sterling Publishing Co., Inc., unless otherwise specified

Distributed in Canada by Sterling Publishing,
c/o Canadian Manda Group, 165 Dufferin Street
Toronto, Ontario, Canada M6K 3H6

Distributed in the United Kingdom by GMC Distribution Services,
Castle Place, 166 High Street, Lewes, East Sussex, England BN7 1XU

Distributed in Australia by Capricorn Link (Australia) Pty Ltd.,
P.O. Box 704, Windsor, NSW 2756 Australia

If you have questions or comments about this book, please contact:
Lark Books
67 Broadway
Asheville, NC 28801
828-253-0467

Manufactured in China

ISBN 13: 978-1-60059-377-2

For information about custom editions, special sales, and premium and corporate purchases, please contact
the Sterling Special Sales Department at 800-805-5489 or specialsales@sterlingpub.com.

For Alan

Contents

Introduction

I really wanted to make some clothes for my daughter when she was born. Many of you have probably wanted to do the same for your girls. The problem was, I didn't learn to sew at my mother's knee. In fact, I never sewed a stitch until I got to college. One day—out of nowhere and for no particular reason—I decided I wanted to learn how to sew, so I bought a machine and tried to make a tablecloth. I say "tried to" because it was surely the worst tablecloth *ever* made.

Never one to give up, I tried making clothes for myself next, but the results were always disappointing, mostly because nothing fit properly. Then my daughter appeared. I made a couple of things with okay results. When I discovered the A-line dress, though, a whole new world opened up before me. The A-line was such a *simple* pattern. It was easy to fit, easy to adapt, and that single flat front piece just begged for fun embellishment. I was hooked.

For years now, I've been making A-line dresses in infinite variations, and I recently realized that *this* is what truly taught me to sew. So now I'm passing these projects on to you. It doesn't matter whether you're a beginning sewer or an experienced seamstress: there's a project or two in this book for you and a little girl you love, whether she's your daughter, granddaughter, niece, or neighbor, girly-girl or tomboy.

I've included some of my favorites in these pages. The reversible Double Duty (page 72) was inspired by a skirt I had as a child—I loved to go into the restroom midday to turn it inside out! The Wrap-a-Rama wrap dress (page 68) was my answer to my daughter's frustration with back zippers and buttons when she wanted to get dressed "all by herself." I designed Getting Ruffled (page 58) because of the dresses that were sometimes already outgrown by the time I got around to doing the boring hemming. And my all-time favorite, The Shirt off Daddy's Back (page 52), allowed me to reuse the buttery soft denim of one of my husband's favorite shirts.

As I started to write this book, I put out a call to other designers to see what they could do with the simple A-line and got even more wonderful ideas than I had hoped for. I had never thought about adding sleeves, but look how lovely they are in Butterfly Wings (page 82)! I've done a lot of appliqué and made a lot of pockets, but it never occurred to me to incorporate the pocket into the appliqué as in Over the Top (page 37)—genius! The gem-encrusted collar added to Bling It On (page 78) is, hands down, my daughter's favorite of the bunch. The tuxedo bib on Puttin' on the Ritz (page 86) looks simply fabulous, and the lovely embroidery in Enchanted Woodland (page 43) has inspired me to start embroidering anything I can fit into a hoop.

The book begins with an overview of basic sewing, followed by directions on how to make the basic A-line dress. The projects are organized into groups of similar techniques (more or less). Just Embellished (which runs on pages 34-51), showcases decorative additions; Making Small Changes (pages 52-74) involves little alterations to the pattern; Layers (pages 75-81) plays with fabric; Adding More (pages 82-89) features additions to the basic pattern; Cutting Up (pages 90-99) divides the pattern into pieces; and Seams Right (pages 100-125) offers some playful alterations to the A-line. As you make the different projects, you'll also be adding new skills to your repertoire. If you stitch up Cross My Heart (page 40), you're going to learn how to do chicken scratch embroidery. Make All Tied Up (page 108), and you'll find out how to create custom piping and add it to a seam. Sew up Peekaboo (page 46) for a lesson in reverse appliqué. All of this will be a cinch because the step-by-step instructions are supplemented with illustrations.

I hope you'll use the basic dress pattern as a starting point, as I did, and then let inspiration guide you. Adapt the A-line to your vision, and you'll be able to use all these techniques to create your own designs and variations. I can't wait to see what you come up with!

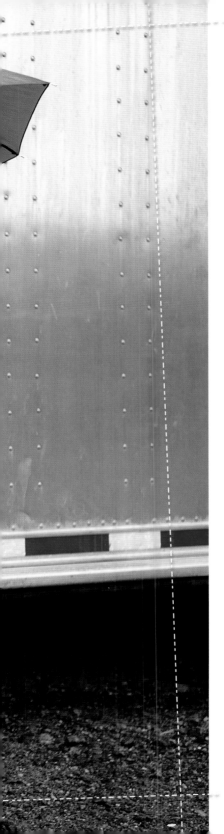

the basics

Tools and Supplies

All you *really* need to make the adorable A-line dresses in this book is fabric and a few simple tools. The short list of things in the box at right will make your sewing life easier and more efficient.

Sewing Machine

Okay, it seems obvious, but I include the sewing machine here so I can talk about what you should look for in a machine. All you need for most sewing is a basic straight stitch. The ability to backstitch at the beginning and end of your stitching is nice, but not absolutely necessary—you can always hand-knot your seams so they don't unravel. A zigzag stitch is also helpful, especially if you like to appliqué or make a lot of buttonholes. Most modern machines can do these stitches. A vintage machine might not, but don't worry; anything other than the basic straight stitch is great if you've got it, but certainly not necessary.

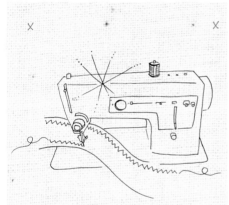

Basic Sewing Kit

Sewing machine and needles
Sewing scissors or shears
Straight pins
Seam ripper
Sewing ruler/hem gauge
Point turner
Vanishing ink fabric marker, chalk, and other marking pens
Spray starch
Iron and ironing board
Thread to match the project

Serger

A serger is a definite bonus when you sew a *lot* of garments, because it seams and finishes the edge in one step, cleanly and quickly. I've been sewing for more than 15 years and I only recently got a serger. Like a fancy sewing machine, it's nice, but by no means necessary.

Scissors

You'll want an assortment of scissors. Small scissors with pointed tips are perfect for snipping threads and clipping curves, but you'll need 7- to 8-inch (17.8 to 20.3 cm) dressmaking shears for cutting the fabric. You'll probably want pinking shears for finishing seams, too.

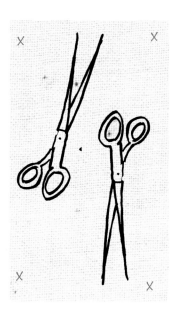

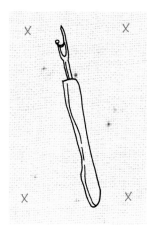

Straight Pins

You'll need lots of straight pins. Those with colored ball heads are easier to spot when you're sewing at full speed, and therefore easier to avoid stitching over.

Seam Ripper

You might think you won't need this, but don't delude yourself. You *will* be ripping out some of your work and nothing does this onerous task better than a seam ripper. I have one at my sewing machine, one at my worktable, one at my ironing board, and one in my traveling kit. I use them a lot.

Sewing Ruler/Hem Gauge

This nifty little ruler with a sliding arrow helps you quickly measure the same distance over and over again. It's perfect for marking a hem. Sure, you could use a regular ruler, but a hem gauge is really inexpensive and you'll be surprised how often you reach for it.

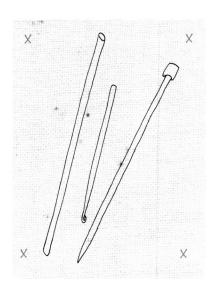

Point Turner

You'll want a point turner. It helps form square corners and angled seams—but don't rush out and buy one. A chopstick is a good substitute, and so is a largish crochet hook or knitting needle. The trick is to find something pointy enough to poke a really crisp corner, but not so pointy that it makes a hole in the fabric.

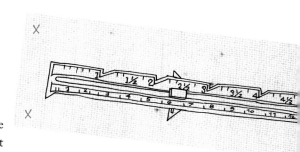

Marking Tools

I love water-soluble markers for transferring pattern markings to fabric. Make your marks and then, when you don't need them anymore, a little spritz of water makes them disappear. Just be careful not to press over the marks or you might heat-set them and make them permanent. Some fabrics are too dark for the marker to show, so keep chalk on hand for those projects.

Spray Starch

Spray starch is very handy for making slippery synthetic fabrics behave, and it's available at the grocery store.

Iron and Ironing Board

You do lots of pressing as you sew, so a sturdy ironing board and an iron that holds a substantial amount of water are essential—you don't want to have to stop to refill your iron with water all the time. This tool is one of your best sewing friends, so take good care of it. I use filtered water in mine to avoid mineral buildup on the plate.

Thread

You might think that choosing thread is pretty easy—just select a color that matches—right? Wrong. When I sewed my very first project I didn't know that there were different kinds of thread. I chose something called buttonhole twist, a very thick, bulky thread that makes a terrible seam. So, take a look at what you're buying—cotton/polyester blend is suitable for most general sewing—and be sure to find and buy thread that is labeled *all-purpose*.

Fabric

Of course you'll need fabric. And choosing fabric for a child's garment is especially exciting, because the possibilities are endless! Ooh—where to start?!

Woven Fabrics

Non-stretchy fabrics (known in the biz as wovens) are the easiest fabrics to work with. They're definitely the best choice for beginners. You don't need any special tools or techniques and, for the most part, they behave nicely. The quilting section of your fabric store will have scads of easy-to-work-with cottons in fabulous prints, but don't stop there. Roam the entire store and let your imagination run wild. How about a cute dress in a tweedy suit fabric? Or a fancy silk dress for a special occasion? Almost any woven fabric is suitable for making A-line dresses.

Machine Washable?

The A-line dress has no gathers or darts or construction details that limit your fabric choices. It's pretty much any woven fabric goes—from the sheerest silk to the woolliest upholstery fabric. Just make sure you can wash it, especially because you're sewing for kids! I once bought a chenille upholstery fabric that indicated it required dry cleaning. It was the perfect color and texture, so I gave it a try. Not only did it stand up through the washer and dryer cycles, but all the stiff sizing washed right out and I was left with a soft, drapey beauty of a fabric. Another similar fabric disintegrated in the wash and I was left with a handful of yarn. You never know until you wash!

If you love a fabric, buy a small swatch, take it home, and wash it just like you plan to wash the finished garment. If the swatch holds up, you can go ahead and use the fabric to make the dress.

Weighty Issues

A-line dresses lend themselves to both lightweight, floaty fabrics like silks and chiffons, and stiffer, heavyweight fabrics, like denim and corduroy. Either weight works, just take care not to mix them in one garment—they don't play well together! A heavyweight fabric will overpower a lightweight one, eliminating all its floatiness. The seams will also probably pucker and the whole thing will just look weird.

You *can* use a lightweight fabric to line a heavyweight dress, but don't mix them together in the dress itself.

Nap Time?

Some of my favorite fabrics are napped fabrics, which means they have a surface texture. You've seen them—the ones most commonly used are velvet and corduroy. They're lovely to touch, but they do require some special handling. When you position the pattern pieces on the fabric, you must make sure that the nap is running in the same direction for all the pieces so the finished garment feels and looks right. Run your hand down the fabric. One direction feels smooth while the other feels rough. I like things to feel smooth when I run my hand from shoulder to hem. You might prefer it the other way around. Either way is fine as long as you're consistent. It sometimes takes a bit more fabric to ensure that all the pieces run in the same direction, so buy extra.

The other tricky thing about napped fabrics is that they tend to creep and slip while you sew—*very* irritating. The solution? Use tons of pins. I pin at *least* every inch (2.5 cm) when I'm sewing with velvet.

Prepare to Sew

Once you've chosen your fabric, you need to take a few more steps before you're ready to stitch up a dress.

Preparing Your Fabric

It's time to do chores. That's right—head to the laundry room. You *must* prewash any fabric and trim (if you're using it) before you sew with them. I've tried to skip this step and the results were definitely not pretty.

Why prewash? It preshrinks the fabric. This is important when you're making clothes that you want to fit, but even if you aren't making clothes, prewashing helps eliminate puckered seams. If you sew before preshrinking, the first time you wash your project the fabric will usually shrink a bit, but your sewing thread won't. This makes your seams look awful. Prewashing also helps remove the ink or dye that might bleed out of the fabric or trim. Consider what happens when you make a white dress with red trim. Correct-a-mundo: the red dye may bleed onto the white fabric. You certainly don't want that to happen, so prewash your fabric and your trim, but wash them separately. Iron your fabric before you cut it.

Determining Pattern Size

Fitting a child for a loose-fitting A-line dress is pretty easy. I've included the chest and height measurements here. The chest measurement is exactly what it sounds like—use a flexible measuring tape and measure around the chest. The easiest way to measure height is to have your child stand straight up against a wall and measure from the floor to the top of the head. Most of the time the chest measurement will point you to one size and the height measurement will point you to another. If that happens, always use the chest measurement to determine the best size and then be prepared to adjust the length of the dress as necessary. It's much easier to change the length of the dress than it is to change the way it fits around the body.

MEASUREMENT CHART						
SIZE	3	4	5	6	7	8
CHEST (IN INCHES)	22	23	24	25	26	27
CHEST (IN CM)	56	58	61	64	66	69
HEIGHT (IN INCHES)	38	41	44	47	50	52
HEIGHT (IN CM)	97	104	112	119	127	132

Bias isn't always a bad thing.

If you look closely at a piece of fabric you can see that the threads of the weave run in two directions. The grainline runs parallel to the selvedge; the other threads run perpendicular to the grainline. If you cut along either of those straight lines (either parallel or perpendicular to the selvedge) you're "cutting on the straight of grain" (figure 1). This makes for fairly stable raw edges.

If you cut at an angle across the fabric it's called "cutting on the bias" (figure 2). These raw edges are easily stretched out of shape. So, for example, until you get all the stitching finished around a curved neckline, be extra careful with your pressing to make sure you don't stretch out that curve. This easy stretchiness can have its advantages. You'll often cut binding strips on the bias—that's why they're sometimes called bias strips—because it's so easy to wrap those strips neatly around a curved edge. They just stretch right around the curve and shape beautifully.

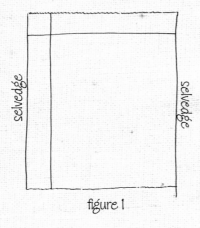

figure 1

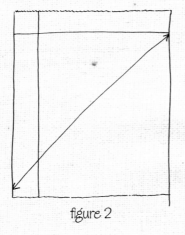

figure 2

Preparing Your Pattern

The first thing you need to do is tedious, but you'll be glad you did it. Trace the pattern pieces onto big sheets of paper, such as tissue paper, wrapping paper, or taped-together copy paper—it doesn't really matter. You can even use muslin. What you don't want to do is cut into the original, pristine multisized pattern. A-line dresses are like potato chips; you can't stop with just one. You're going to want to make changes to the pattern, and your child is going to grow. So trace just the size that you intend to use and keep the original pattern as a master copy.

How to trace? The best way is with a light source behind the paper. Some people have fancy light boxes, but I think a window works great. Tape your pattern to a window and your paper over the pattern. Trace the outline of the pattern and the internal markings with a thick black marker. Be sure to copy all the markings and helpful information, including the grainline arrow (see sidebar at left), which you'll need to lay out the pattern pieces on the fabric. Cut each pattern piece along the exterior line.

Fabric Layout and Cutting

Lay your fabric out on a large, flat surface. If the pattern indicates to cut it on the fabric fold, then fold your fabric lengthwise—that is, with the selvedges (the clean, finished edges) together. Lay your pattern pieces so that the grainline arrow is parallel to the selvedge. This will keep your dress hanging the right way. Have you ever worn jeans that felt twisty somehow? That's because they weren't cut with the fabric on the straight grain—it's annoying and easy to prevent.

To keep the pattern from shifting on top of the fabric, most people use pins, but I prefer pattern weights. You can buy them at a fabric store, but I make my own with a bag of fish tank gravel and small zip-top bags. They're small, inexpensive, and easy to shape around curves. I love them.

Cut out all your pattern pieces and transfer the construction markings with a fabric marking pen or chalk.

You're ready to sew!

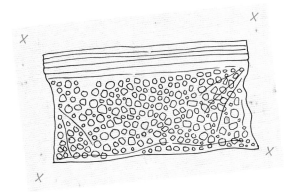

Overview of sewing techniques

Throughout the project instructions you'll find much of the same lingo used over and over again. You don't need special skills to make these dresses, just a basic understanding of the most common sewing machine techniques.

Machine Stitches

Every sewing machine is a little different, so refer to your owner's manual for a refresher course on stitch adjustment. Adjusting the stitch length for a longer stitch creates a basting stitch, and adjusting the stitch width can produce some cool, decorative zigzag stitches. Practice stitching on a swatch of the fabric that you'll be using to make sure the thread tension and stitch length and width are correct.

Backstitch

Backstitching is just like it sounds—you take a couple of stitches backward at the beginning and end of seams and most other stitching. It works like a knot to keep the thread ends from unraveling.

Baste

Basting is temporary stitching. It holds layers in place until you're ready to stitch them, or it gathers a length of fabric. It's the longest machine stitch and the easiest to rip out when you don't need it anymore. I usually don't backstitch at the beginning and end of basting because backstitching makes it harder to remove the stitches.

Edgestitch

Edgestitching is a finishing stitch taken as close as possible to a folded edge.

Staystitch

Staystitching is a row of standard-length straight stitches (about 10 stitches per inch [2.5 cm]) taken through a single thickness of fabric in the seam allowance. By stitching in the seam allowance, the stitching isn't visible on the finished garment and you don't have to rip the stitches out. Staystitching is usually done along a curved edge, such as the neckline, to prevent it from stretching during construction.

Topstitch

Topstitching is decorative stitching on the outside (or top—get it?) of a finished garment. It adds a more casual, sporty look and is often done with novelty thread or a contrasting color.

Zigzag Stitch

You'll use this stitch to clean finish the cut edges of seam allowances and to edgestitch appliqué embellishments. You can shorten the stitch so it looks like a stack of straight lines (or a satin stitch) instead of a zigzag when you're stitching appliqués, or you can widen the stitch so it's really open. Finesse the stitch setting to get the effect you want.

Hand Stitches

You'll want to use a machine for most of your basic sewing, but handwork is great for embellishment and necessary for some finishing work. It's also an extremely pleasant way to spend an evening on the couch—especially if there's a crackling fire in front of you.

Ladder Stitch

The ladder stitch or slip stitch is my all-time favorite hand stitch. If you're looking for a nearly invisible stitch, this is it. I use it to sew an opening closed, to finish the opening in a lining, for appliqué, and lots more.

1 If you're sewing a seam closed, press the seam allowances open so you have nice crisp folds along the seamline. The folds will act as a guide for your stitches.

2 Thread your needle and knot the end (see page 23). Insert your needle inside the item, so the thread knot is inside (figure 3). Bring the needle out through one of the folds, close to the opening.

3 Insert your needle into the fold directly across the opening from where your thread came out. Let the needle travel under and along the fold for ¼ inch (6 mm) or less (figure 3). Push the needle out through the fold.

4 For each subsequent stitch, the thread should jump straight across the opening and run hidden inside the pressed seam allowance fold, like a ladder—hence the name (figure 4). Repeat until you've finished closing the seam.

5 Pull the stitches tight so they disappear. Even if you sew with black thread on white fabric you won't see these stitches—I promise. Tie off the end of your thread and you're done!

Ladder-Stitch Appliqué

I made this term up, but it works.

1 Before you cut the appliqué out of your chosen fabric, cut a piece of freezer paper the same shape as the appliqué. Iron the freezer paper to the back of the appliqué fabric (use a press cloth to protect your iron). Cut the appliqué from the fabric, including about ¼ inch (6 mm) extra all around to ensure a clean finished edge.

2 Work at the ironing board and use the freezer paper as a guide to carefully wrap the extra ¼ inch (6 mm) of fabric over the edge of the freezer paper. Press well; apply spray starch if the fabric doesn't form a nice, sharp crease around the outside edge. *(continued on next page)*

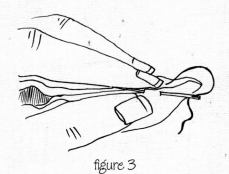

figure 3

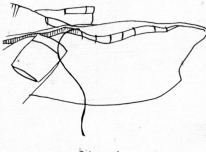

figure 4

3 Remove the freezer paper. It worked well as a guide, but now that you have a nice clean shape with all the turned edges crisply pressed in place, you don't need it anymore.

4 Pin the appliqué to the base fabric.

5 Sew the appliqué to the fabric using the ladder stitch described above. The "top" stitches will run through the folded edge of the appliqué piece, just like they ran through the fold of the seam allowance. The "bottom" stitches will simply run under the base fabric.

Seams

Unless you're instructed otherwise, the seams in this book are made with straight stitches, set at 8 to 12 stitches per inch (2.5 cm), and ⅝-inch (1.6 cm) seam allowances. After you sew your seams, clip the curves and press the stitches to make sure the seams are smooth and pucker free.

Clipping Curves

Any time you sew a curved seam you need to clip small notches in your seam allowance. Never skip this step! On a concave curved seam, the raw edge of the fabric is shorter than the stitched seam, so when you turn the garment right side out, that shorter raw edge doesn't fully open up to the curve. The solution is to clip small snips in the seam allowance, from the raw edge right up to (but not into!) the line of stitching. If it's a tight curve, clip every ¼ inch (6 mm). If it's a gentle curve, you can spread your snips out to about every inch (2.5 cm). When you turn the garment right side out, the snips will allow the seam allowance to spread open like a fan and you'll end up with beautiful, smooth curves.

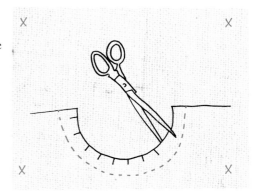

Press or Iron?

Ah. . .another mystery of the sewing world. There's actually a difference between pressing and ironing. Ironing involves sliding the iron back and forth. It's what you do to prewashed fabric and to finished garments to remove wrinkles.

Pressing is what you do to every seam as you sew. It makes the stitches sink into the fabric and it makes your seams flat and smooth.

To properly press a seam you don't move the iron back and forth. Instead, you carefully open your garment, smooth the newly sewn seam flat as best you can with your fingers, and then press the iron into the seam. If the fabric can handle it, give it a shot of steam. Then lift the iron and move it to the next section of the seam that needs pressing.

This might seem nitpicky and weird, but it's actually very important. Without the stabilizing effect of seams and hems, ironing can stretch the edges and distort the shape of a piece of fabric.

Turn and Press

"Turn and press" is one of the most ubiquitous phrases in pattern-speak, and it was completely mystifying to me when I started to sew. Huh? Turn what? Where? Press? With what? It's actually pretty simple: *turn* your garment right side out and *press* the seam flat. If you want your sewing to look good, you need to press every seam right after you sew it. Sometimes the pattern instructions will tell you to press the seams open or toward a particular side. If it doesn't specify, then always press both seam allowances to one side—preferably toward the back of the garment.

Embroidery Stitches

There are a lot of fresh, new approaches to embroidery making the rounds on the Internet lately—and I've fallen in love all over again. Those colors! That quiet, peaceful stitching! Those colors! I kind of want to add embroidery to everything I own, and so do some of the designers in this book, who added embroidery to their dresses. Here are some of the most common stitches.

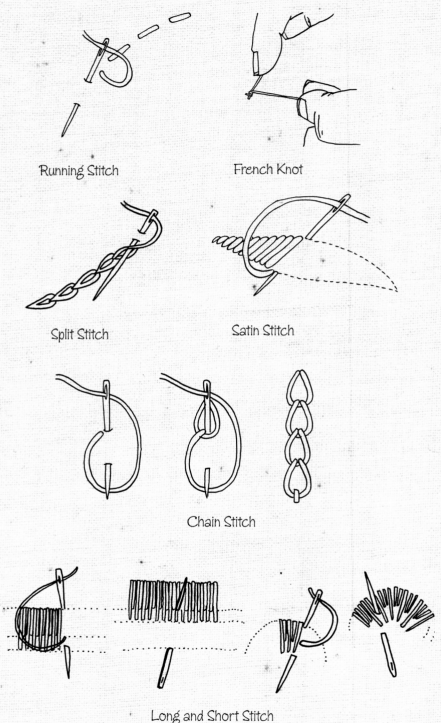

Running Stitch

French Knot

Split Stitch

Satin Stitch

Chain Stitch

Long and Short Stitch

Most Awesome Knot Ever

I give many thanks to my mother-in-law for teaching me how to work this knot. I always feel like such a pro when I use this in public. I've actually had people do a double-take and ask me how I do that—it's that awesome.

1 Thread your needle.

2 Hold the eye of the needle in your right hand with the tip pointing toward the left. With your left hand, hold the end of the thread so it points toward the right (figure 5).

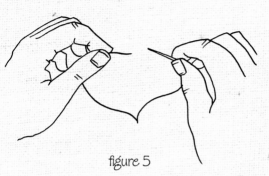

figure 5

3 Pinch the tail end of the thread against the needle with your right hand, and wrap the tail end of the thread four or five times around the needle (figure 6).

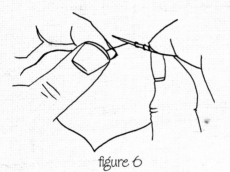

figure 6

4 Using your left hand, pinch the wrapped thread tight around the needle. Use your right hand to pull the needle through your left-handed pinch (figure 7). Keep the wrapped thread pinched tight as you draw the needle, and then the thread, through the wrapped coils. When you get to the end of the thread, the coils will magically make a knot.

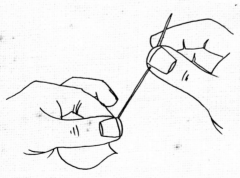

figure 7

Seam Finishes

Finish your work!? What difference does it make if you finish the cut edges of your seams? They're on the inside of the garment where nobody will see them, right? Well, sort of. The sewing police won't come and get you if you leave your seams unfinished, but the garment you worked so hard to make won't last as long. The inside will look terrible the first time you wash it; the agitation of the sewing machine creates jagged edges, loose strings, and thread dreadlocks. It's quite possible your little person will refuse to wear your beautiful creation because the stringy threads make her feel like there are spiders crawling inside her dress. It's not difficult to finish seams and it's totally worth the effort.

Serging

The quickest and easiest way to finish seam allowances is with a serger. Just run the edge of the seam allowances through the serger; it trims the edges and forms an overlock stitch all in one step. It's the finish you see inside almost all store-bought clothes.

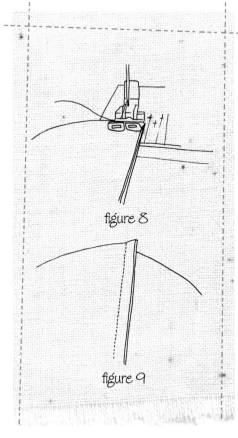

figure 8

figure 9

Stitch and Pink

This is almost as easy as using a serger. After you sew a seam, run another line of stitching in the seam allowances, about ¼ inch (6 mm) away from the seamline. Trim away the excess seam allowance close to the second line of stitching with pinking shears. The pinking shears leave a soft, fluffy, comfortable edge after washing.

French Seam

A French seam is a fancy seam and seam finish all in one; it's not very hard and you end up with beautifully finished seams. Allow for a standard ⅝-inch (1.6 cm) seam allowance. It works best with sheer or flimsy fabrics and *very* gentle curves.

1 Sew your seam with the *wrong* sides of the fabric together and a ⅜-inch (1 cm) seam allowance. If you have any sewing experience, this feels wrong, but trust me.

2 Trim away any excess seam allowance—you only want to leave about ⅛ inch (3 mm).

3 Turn your garment inside out (the right sides should be together now) and press. The itty-bitty ⅛-inch (3 mm) seam allowance should be sandwiched between the two layers of fabric.

4 Sew the seam again, this time using a ¼-inch (6 mm) seam allowance (figure 8). Turn the garment right side out and press. The raw edges are encased between the two rows of stitching (figure 9). Pretty elegant, eh?

Bias Binding

Wrapping a strip of bias fabric over a raw fabric edge is a beautiful way to clean finish the edge. It can be done inside on seams that don't show, or on the outside of the garment for an added design feature. You can buy pre-made bias tape, but it's easy to make your own so it matches or complements the dress perfectly.

There are several ways to attach bias binding; it can be done in one step or in multiple steps. Refer to the project instructions for how to attach the bias to the garment and the instructions below for how to make bias binding.

1 The bias grainline is a 45° angle to the selvage. Cut strips of fabric four times (for double fold) or two times (for single fold) as wide as your desired bias tape, parallel to the bias grainline (figure 10).

2 You might need to piece several strips to get the length you need. To do so, place the end of one strip over the other at a right angle with the right sides together. Stitch diagonally from one corner to the opposite corner of the overlapping squares (figure 11).

3 Cut off the corners, leaving a ¼-inch (6 mm) seam allowance (figure 12). Open up and press the allowances flat. Refer to the project instructions for how to press and apply the bias binding.

figure 10

figure 11

figure 12

Garment closures

Finally, some closure! For years I didn't make clothing because I was terrified of fastening mechanisms—especially zippers and buttons. Then, when I started making clothes I only made things that used elastic (Ha ha! No closures!) or patterns that could be adapted to use hook-and-loop tape. Seriously. It was a long time before I was daring enough to try a zipper, and even longer before I braved buttonholes. It is my sincerest hope that you won't delay closure—I'll show you how.

Elastic

I use elastic to make the loops for buttonholes (see page 28). The only thing I'm going to tell you about elastic is to *always* pre-stretch it. Just pull it out of the package and stretch it as much as possible. Do this *before* you measure it—the difference can be significant.

Snaps

I love snaps. They're easy to apply and they have a nice, clean look. The method for attaching them is different for each brand, but they all have instructions on the package.

Snap Tape

Even cooler than snaps is sew-on snap tape. It's often used on baby garments (to allow easy access for diapering), but there's no reason to save it just for babies. Besides its intended use as a closure, it's also a great way to attach fancy trim that should be removed for laundering.

Hook and Eye

This closure is almost as easy to apply as snaps. Just sew the hook to one side of the opening and the eye to the other. They're tiny—the hardest part is simply holding on to them.

Zippers

Once I learned how easy it is to install a zipper, it became my favorite closure—much better than hook-and-loop tape. Always place the zipper in a seam. For the A-line dresses in this book, the zipper will be in the center back seam. However, there's no reason you can't alter the pattern (after reading this book) to move the zipper to a front seam.

1 Pin the two fabric pieces together as if to stitch the seam. Lay the zipper on the pieces so that the top of the zipper pull is ⅝ inch (1.6 cm) from the top edge of the fabric. Mark the bottom (metal stop) of the zipper on the fabric with a pin or fabric-marking pen (figure 13). Remove the zipper.

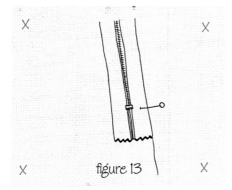

figure 13

2 Beginning at the bottom of the dress, sew the seam, using a regular stitch length, up to the marked spot. Backstitch and then adjust the machine stitch length to a basting stitch. Continue stitching the rest of the seam up to the top edge. Do not backstitch at the top.

3 Press the seam open. With the wrong side of the fabric facing up, and the right side of the zipper facing down, pin the zipper so that the teeth are centered over the basted seam and the bottom zipper stop is at the marked location.

4 Install a zipper presser foot on your sewing machine—it allows you to stitch very close to the teeth of the zipper. Working from the wrong side and using the zipper tape as a guide, stitch down one side of the zipper, across the bottom, and up the other side.

5 Use your seam ripper to rip out just the basting stitches (figure 14).

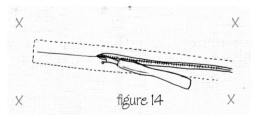

figure 14

Congratulations! Now you can zip and unzip the garment and you have fancy little flaps that keep the zipper neatly covered! You may now dispose of your hook-and-loop tape.

Button Variations:

Okay, I get that making buttonholes is intimidating, so I'm going to ease you into the idea of button closures with a couple of simple substitutes. You can't use the next two closures for the front of a dress, where you need the two sides to overlap. For overlapping pieces, you'll need to bite the bullet and make regular buttonholes (or chicken out and use snaps). But for the back of a dress (particularly for the A-line dresses in this book), you can use these easy buttonhole substitutes.

Elastic Loop Buttonhole

When you sew the top corner of the back of the dress, tie elastic cord into a little loop (wrap the cord around your button to determine the right length) and catch it in the seam of the dress. Figure 15 shows you how you should orient it when placing it between the back piece and the lining. When you turn the garment right side out, the loop will be sticking out of the seam, ready to hold on to a button. The knotted end is hidden in the seam allowance.

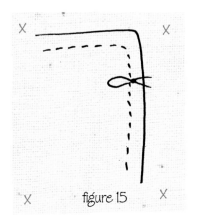

figure 15

Wrapped Thread Loop

This closure is slightly fancier (and more work) than the elastic loop; however, it offers the advantage of being made *after* the dress is finished—you don't have to remember to do it during the dress construction, as with the elastic loop. Sew three or four threads to make a loop at the edge of the garment. Wrap those threads with side-by-side knots (it's just like a tiny macramé project), so they're completely covered and become a nice, strong cord (figure 16).

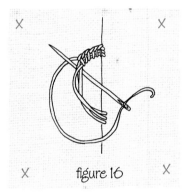

figure 16

Machine-Stitched Buttonholes

Okay, now for the real buttonhole. You'll be surprised at how straightforward it really is. It may, in fact, become your very favorite closure. There are so many beautiful buttons to choose from that you should want to learn how to make a buttonhole. I've tried various buttonhole attachments and automatic buttonhole features on the machines I've owned. None of them has worked very well, but I get great results when I make buttonholes manually.

1 Mark the placement of the buttonhole by placing the button on the garment at the desired location. Mark a line that resembles the letter I under the middle of the button. Add little dashes at each end to mark the buttonhole length (figure 17). If you're sewing on lightly colored fabric, mark it with a water-soluble marker. If you're working with a dark fabric, sew the marking directly onto the fabric with light-colored thread. It's important that you be able to clearly see the line and length markings, so you know where to start and stop sewing.

2 Set your machine to a narrow zigzag or satin stitch. Beginning at the top of the I (figure 18), sew just to the right of the vertical line. Stop when you get to the bottom, making sure your needle will swing to the left when you resume stitching.

3 Adjust the stitch width so it's slightly more than twice as wide as the satin stitch you used in step 2. Take a few stitches across the bottom of the I (figure 19). Stop stitching with the needle down in the lower left-hand corner of the I.

4 Lift the presser foot and turn the garment around 180°. Adjust the stitch width back to the narrow width. Sew down what is now the right side of the vertical line. Stop at the bottom so that the needle will swing to the left when you resume stitching (figure 20).

figure 17

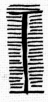

figure 18

figure 19

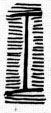

figure 20

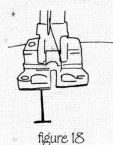

figure 21

5 Adjust the stitch width back to the wider setting. Take a few stitches to complete the buttonhole (figure 21). Pull the top thread to the wrong side, knot it, and trim the thread ends. You will have created a long, thin rectangle of satin stitching with no stitching in the center.

6 *Very carefully,* cut open the center of the buttonhole. I like to use the seam ripper to cut each end, working toward the center to avoid cutting through the stitches. Then I use small sharp scissors to finish cutting the buttonhole open.

7 If the fabric frays, dab the cut edges with liquid seam sealant. *Voilà!* You've made a buttonhole!

Notes

X If your fabric is lightweight, position a piece of stabilizer paper or interfacing under the buttonhole area while you sew the buttonhole. It helps support the fabric and keeps it from stretching. You can trim the paper away after you finish the buttonhole.

X Always make a practice buttonhole on scrap fabric to see whether you want or need to adjust the width of the stitches or the length of the buttonhole.

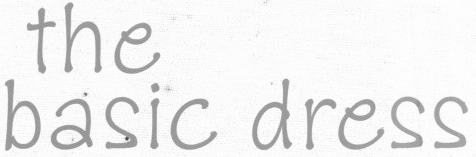

the basic dress

The following instructions tell you how to make the basic A-line dress using the pattern provided in the envelope at the back of this book. Every project in this book is a variation on this basic dress, so you'll refer back to these instructions frequently.

What You Need

X **Basic Sewing Kit (page 11)**

X **Basic Pattern**

X **Fabric** (Refer to Yardage Chart)

X **1 button**

Seam allowances:
⅝ **inch (1.6 cm) unless otherwise noted**

What You Do

1 Trace or cut out the four pattern pieces—dress front, dress back, facing front, and facing back—in the desired size. Lay the pieces on your fabric and cut them out.

2 Staystitch (page 18) the curved front and back neck edges, ½ inch (1.3 cm) from the cut edge. This helps stabilize the edge so the fabric doesn't stretch.

Yardage Chart

		SIZE 3	SIZE 4	SIZE 5	SIZE 6	SIZE 7	SIZE 8
MAIN FABRIC	45" (1.1 m) wide	1 yd (90 cm)	1⅛ yd (1 m)	1⅛ yd (1 m)	1¼ yd (1.1 m)	1½ yd (1.4 m)	1¾ yd (1.6 m)
	60" (1.5 m) wide	⅞ yd (80 cm)	⅞ yd (80 cm)	1 yd (90 cm)	1 yd (90 cm)	1 yd (90 cm)	1⅛ yd (1 m)

3 Stitch the front of the dress to the back of the dress at the shoulder seams with the right sides of the fabric together.

4 Stitch the front facing to the back facings at the shoulder seams with the right sides of the fabric together.

5 Narrow hem the bottom of the front and back facings (see Tip box). To sew a standard narrow hem, press the edge ¼ inch (6 mm) to the wrong side and then ¼ inch (6 mm) to the wrong side again. Edgestitch (page 18) close to the inside folded edge.

6 Pin and stitch the facing to the neck and armhole edges of the dress with the right sides together, matching the shoulder seams, center front, and center back (figure 1). Trim the seam allowances to roughly ¼ inch (6 mm) wide and clip the curves (page 20).

7 Turn the dress right side out by gently pulling each back piece through each shoulder, underneath the facing. Depending on the size of the dress, it can be tricky to get those back pieces started through the shoulder seams. Try attaching a large safety pin to one corner of the back piece; use it to lead the fabric through the narrow shoulder opening.

8 After you've turned the dress right side out, roll the neckline and armhole seams between your thumb and fingers so the facing doesn't show on the outside of the dress. Press the seams.

9 At the armholes, extend the facing up from the dress. Pin the front to the back at each side seam with the right sides together in one continuous seam from the bottom of the dress up over the seam to the hemmed edge of the facing. Sew the seams as pinned (figure 2).

(continued on next page)

Tip

Narrow hems can cause frustration and burned fingers, so here's a neat trick. Sew a line of straight stitching ¼ inch (6 mm) from the cut edge. The stitching will act as a pressing guide, so fold the hem to the wrong side along the stitching and press. Avoid singed fingers by using the point of your seam ripper to hold the hem in place as you press. Fold this newly pressed edge ¼ inch (6 mm) to the inside, using the pressed fold as your guide. Press again, then stitch the hem in place. Of course, if you have a serger you can always serge the raw edge.

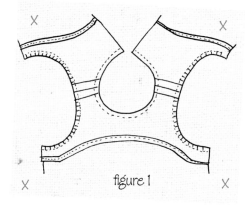

figure 1

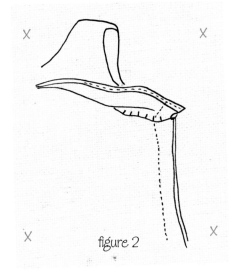

figure 2

Tip

Facings are a nice (and easy) way to make the inside of your dress look finished. Usually they lie flat on their own, but if you want to make sure they stay in place, tack them to the dress at the side and shoulder seams with a couple of hand stitches. Consider using a contrasting fabric for the facing. It's a little extra flair for no extra work.

10 Press the side seams toward the back of the dress. Fold the facing back down and press.

11 Extend the facing at the center back like you did for the side seams, so it doesn't get caught in the seam. Sew the center back seam starting at the bottom edge of the dress and stopping at the large dot. Backstitch (page 18) at the large dot. Turn the dress right side out.

12 Fold the facing back down so that the facing and the dress are right sides together. The top back corners are inside out, but the rest of the dress isn't. Sew from one top edge of the dress to the large dot—the same dot where the back seam stitching ends. Backstitch at the dot. Repeat for the other side of the dress (figure 3).

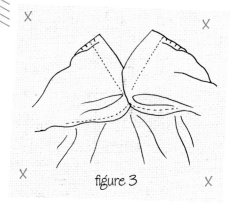

figure 3

13 Diagonally trim away each top corner seam allowance. Turn the facings to the inside of the dress and press.

14 The lower edge of the facings at the center back need to be joined together. Pin the raw edges with the right sides together. Stitch from the bottom of the facing to the large dot (the same dot where all your other stitching comes together). Backstitch, then press the seam open. If it's easier for you, you can always sew that last seam by hand.

15 Try the dress on the child and mark the desired hem length. Cut the dress 1 inch (2.5 cm) longer than the marked length. Turn the bottom of the dress under ½ inch (1.3 cm) and press. Turn it under ½ inch (1.3 cm) again and stitch close to the folded edge. Press the hem once more after stitching.

16 Sew a button to one side of the back opening. Make a wrapped thread loop (page 28) opposite the button so you can button the dress closed.

the
projects

Kids have been playing with felt books and boards for ages. Here's a felt garden of snap-on flowers they can wear around! Make flowers in every shape and color and let your child rearrange them after every washing.

What You Need

X **Basic Sewing Kit (page 11)**

X **Basic Pattern**

X **Flower Templates (page 126)**

X **Fabric (Refer to Yardage Chart for Basic Dress on page 30)**

X **Felt remnants in a variety of colors for flowers**

X **1 button**

X **Snaps and snap-setting kit**

Seam allowances:

⅝ inch (1.6 cm) unless otherwise noted

Shown in size 4

Floral Arrangements

What You Do

Make the Dress and Flowers

1 Make the dress according to the basic instructions (page 30).

2 Use the templates to trace and cut out as many flowers as you like from the felt remnants. The number of flowers depends on the size of the dress. Why not make extra to give your budding designer lots of choices?

3 Arrange and rearrange the flowers on the dress until you're happy with the layout. Following the snap kit package instructions, attach one part of the snap first to the circular top and then to the lower shaped part of each flower and the other part to the dress. Snap the flowers onto the dress.

Tips

x 100% wool felt makes especially nice flowers.

x Remove the flowers to wash the dress and snap them back on in a new configuration after it's been laundered. Be prepared—the wearer may want to redesign her dress several times during the day!

Designer Wendi Gratz

Note

Don't limit yourself to flowers.
How about silly faces? Favorite
animals? Simple polka dots?
Or try a different arrangement.
The felt pieces don't need to be
scattered all over the front of the
dress—a row around the hem or
a stripe down the center front
would look terrific. And here's a
secret—you don't even have to
make the dress. This technique
is a great way to embellish a
purchased dress, or disguise
stains on a hand-me-down.

This tall giraffe appliqué is just perfect for embellishing the whole front of an A-line dress. He's even more perfect when you realize his body is a pocket!

What You Need

X Basic Sewing Kit (page 11)

X Basic Pattern

X Appliqué Templates (page 127)

X Fabric (Refer to Yardage Chart for Basic Dress on page 30)

X ¼ yard (22.9 cm) of paper-backed fusible adhesive

X ¼ yard (22.9 cm) of appliqué fabric

X ⅛ yard (11.4 cm) of cream-colored felt

X Brown yarn

X 1 button

X Hand-sewing needle with large eye

Seam allowances:
⅝ inch (1.6 cm) unless otherwise noted

Shown in size 6

Over the Top

What You Do

Make the Dress and Appliqué

1 Cut out all the dress pattern pieces according to the basic instructions on page 30.

2 Enlarge the giraffe template pieces as indicated. (Depending on the size of the dress you're making, you may want to change the enlargement percentage a little.) Trace them onto the paper side of the fusible adhesive. Trace the giraffe head/neck exactly as it is because the image is already reversed. Following the manufacturer's instructions, fuse the adhesive to the back of the appliqué fabric. Cut out all the pieces and remove the paper backing.

3 Arrange the pieces on the front of the dress. Remove all but the head/neck piece and fuse it in place. Zigzag stitch around the head/neck.

Designer Betsy Couzins

37

4 Lay everything out again and remove all but one leg. Fuse that leg in place and zigzag stitch around it. Repeat until all the legs are fused and stitched in place (figure 1).

5 Fuse the body/pocket piece to the felt and cut it out. Zigzag stitch the fabrics together, across the top of the pocket. Pin the pocket to the dress and zigzag stitch around the curve. Position, fuse, and zigzag the tail in place.

6 Refer to the stitch diagrams on page 22 to embroider the details on the giraffe with the hand-sewing needle and brown yarn (figure 2).

7 Sew the dress together following the basic instructions on page 30. Take a trip to the zoo to celebrate!

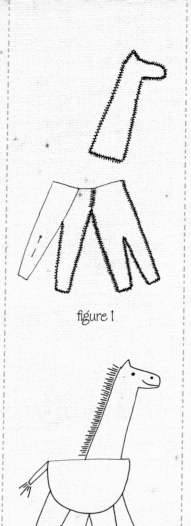

figure 1

figure 2

Note

Now that you've made such a cute dress, you may get requests for more favorite animals. If you're not confident about your drawing abilities, look at coloring books for a simple outline drawing. Or—even better—ask your child to draw you exactly what she wants!

Designer *Betsy Couzins*

What do you get when you mix gingham with cross-stitch? A fun and easy embroidery technique called chicken scratch—and this super-sweet dress.

What You Need

X Basic Sewing Kit (page 11)

X Basic Pattern

X Embroidery Template (page 129)

X Gingham fabric (Refer to Yardage Chart for Basic Dress on page 30)

X 1 button

X 1 skein of matching or contrasting embroidery floss

X Embroidery hoop

X Hand embroidery needle

Seam allowances:
⅝ inch (1.6 cm) unless otherwise noted

Shown in size 6

Cross My Heart

What You Do

Make the Dress

1 Make the dress according to the basic instructions, steps 1 through 16 (page 30).

2 Count the rows in the gingham plaid up from the hem to determine the desired placement of the hand-stitched border. Pin mark the chosen bottom row for the embroidery. The nice thing about using gingham is that the weave of the fabric acts as the grid.

3 Place the embroidery hoop over the right side seam at the border placement pin marking. You'll want to use an embroidery hoop so your stitches don't pull the fabric too tight.

4 Follow the diagram on the embroidery template to embroider the border. You can work each X one at a time or you can work in rows. To work in rows, stitch all your forward slashes in one row and then turn the fabric over and stitch forward slashes again in the same row to complete the X in each box. Be careful to stitch your finishing slashes slanted in the same direction. You'd be surprised how noticeable it is when you don't follow this step. As you finish each section, move the embroidery hoop until you have stitched across the dress. Press well. Tell your little girl that every *X* you've embroidered represents a kiss just for her.

Note

Got the itch for more of this cool embellishment? Well, then, hit the Internet! Chicken scratch is coming back into fashion and there are a lot of free patterns online. Just think— you can embroider a whole wardrobe full of dresses!

Tip

If you're worried about the threads on the inside of the dress snagging or pulling loose in the wash, fuse a piece of lightweight interfacing over the embroidery, inside the dress. This will protect the stitching. Follow the manufacturer's fusing instructions.

Embellish a simple dress with a fanciful group of forest creatures. A few easy embroidery stitches are all you need to make fantasy become reality.

What You Need

X Basic Sewing Kit (page 11)

X Basic Pattern

X Embroidery Template (page 129)

X Fabric (refer to the chart on page 45)

X Transfer paper

X Assorted embroidery floss

X 1 hook-and-eye closure

X Embroidery hoop

X Hand embroidery needle

X Hand-sewing needle and thread

Seam allowances:

⅝ inch (1.6 cm) unless otherwise noted

Shown in size 3

Enchanted Woodland

What You Do

Prepare and Embroider the Dress Front

1 Cut the dress front and back pattern pieces from both the dress and the lining fabrics. Don't cut the facings. Measure and cut away 1 inch (2.5 cm) from the bottom of the lining pattern pieces.

Note

Embroidery is portable, inexpensive, and loads of fun. Best of all, once you master a few basic stitches you can embellish just about anything. Designs are everywhere. Actual patterns are available in books and online, but don't overlook the inspiration that's all around you—fabric designs, the borders on notepads and stationery, grocery store packaging, your child's drawings—if you can trace it, you can embroider it.

Designer Aimee Ray

43

Tip
The markings from transfer paper tend to rub off easily, so I recommend transferring one motif at a time, embroidering it, then transferring the next part of the design.

2 Before you embroider the front dress fabric, machine baste, using contrasting thread, all around the front of the piece, ⅝ inch (1.6 cm) from the cut edges. This will mark the visible part of your dress so none of your beautiful embroidery ends up buried in the seams (figure 1).

figure 1

3 Transfer the embroidery template to the dress front. The easiest transfer method for most fabrics is to tape the embroidery pattern to a window and then tape the fabric over the pattern, and trace it with a disappearing ink or water-soluble fabric marker. If the dress is made from a heavy or dark fabric, like this lovely brown velvet dress, the pattern won't show through the fabric, so you'll have to use transfer paper instead. Follow the instructions that come with the transfer paper; it's much like carbon paper.

4 You can use any embroidery stitches you like (page 22). The split stitch and chain stitch both make a nice, heavy outline. The satin stitch works well for filling in shapes smoothly. If you want a furry-looking finish, use the long and short stitch. Little straight stitches make lovely hedgehog prickles.

Make the Dress

1 Sew the dress following the basic instructions on page 30, substituting the lining pieces for the facings. Hem the lining and the dress separately. Make the lining a bit shorter than the outer dress. Sew the hook and eye at the back neck closing. Admire your work and make plans to add embroidery to your own jeans.

	SIZE 3	SIZE 4	SIZE 5	SIZE 6	SIZE 7	SIZE 8
MAIN FABRIC	¾ yd (68.6 cm)	1 yd (0.9 m)	1 yd (0.9 m)	1 yd (0.9 m)	1 yd (0.9 m)	1 yd (0.9 m)
LINING	¾ yd (68.6 cm)	1 yd (0.9 m)	1 yd (0.9 m)	1 yd (0.9 m)	1 yd (0.9 m)	1 yd (0.9 m)
Yardage is the same for all fabric widths.						

A little reverse appliqué goes a long way toward making a dress extra special. Unlike traditional appliqué, this technique results in a delightfully different "peekaboo" effect.

What You Need

✗ Basic Sewing Kit (page 11)

✗ Basic Pattern

✗ Petal Template (page 129)

✗ Fabric (Refer to Yardage Chart for Basic Dress on page 30)

✗ ½ yard (45.7 cm) of printed appliqué fabric

✗ 1 button, 1⅛ inches (2.9 cm) in diameter for flower center

✗ 1 button, 1⅜ inches (3.5 cm) in diameter for flower center

✗ 1 button for closure

✗ Disappearing-ink fabric marker

✗ Sharp, pointed scissors

Seam allowances:
⅝ inch (1.6 cm) unless otherwise noted

Shown in size 8

Peekaboo

What You Do

Make the Dress

1 Cut out all of the dress pattern pieces according to the basic instructions (page 30).

2 Make two copies of the petal template—one at 200 percent and one at 300 percent. (You may want to adjust the size depending on the size of the dress you're making.) Cut out the template paper pieces and arrange them on the front of the dress. Once you're satisfied with the placement, pin them in place.

3 Cut two pieces of appliqué fabric, each large enough to cover one of the template arrangements completely. Set one piece of appliqué fabric aside and lay the other piece right side up on your work area.

4 Lay the dress front, also with the right side up, over the appliqué fabric so that there's appliqué fabric under each petal of the template, with fabric to spare around all the pieces. Pin the layers together.

5 Trace around the first petal with the marker, and remove that template piece. Carefully narrow zigzag stitch over the line you just traced and press. Repeat for each of the five petals (figure 1).

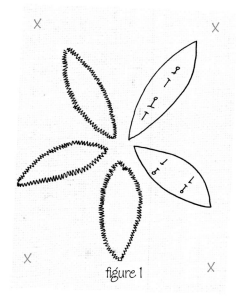

figure 1

6 Once you've sewn all five petals of the first flower, flip the dress front over and trim away the extra appliqué fabric close to the stitching (the fabric outside the petal stitching) as shown in figure 2.

7 Repeat steps 4 through 6 for the second flower.

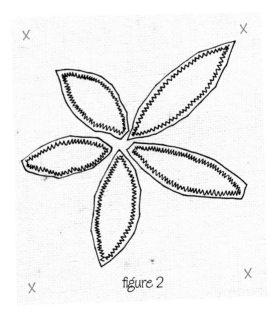

figure 2

8 From the right side, trim away the dress fabric just inside the stitching line of each of the petals. Use your fingers to pull the dress fabric away from the appliqué fabric and with small, sharp scissors, carefully make a small cut in the middle of the petal. Insert the scissors into that cut and trim closely but carefully around the inside of the stitching line (figure 3). Be very careful not to cut the stitching threads or the appliqué fabric.

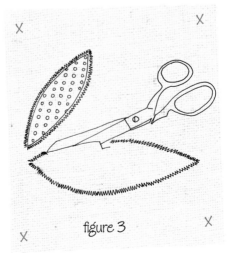

figure 3

9 Press the dress front. Sew the buttons in the center of each of the petal clusters. Follow the basic instructions on page 30 to make the dress.

Tip

If you like this technique and think you'll do more of it, consider investing in a pair of appliqué scissors. The top blade has a sharp point like regular scissors, but the bottom blade has a smooth rounded tip that's perfect for sliding against the lower appliqué fabric without accidentally cutting it.

A patchwork appliqué pocket is the perfect way to use pretty scraps of fabric and add an unexpected splash of color. It's a great place to keep teeny treasures, too.

What You Need

X **Basic Sewing Kit (page 11)**

X **Basic Pattern**

X **Petal and Flower Center Templates (page 127)**

X **Fabric (Refer to Yardage Chart for Basic Dress on page 30)**

X **5-inch (12.7 cm) squares of 6 different pink, yellow, and white petal fabrics**

X **9-inch (22.9 cm) square of pocket lining fabric**

X **3-inch (7.6 cm) square of orange patterned fabric for flower center**

X **1 button**

X **Yellow embroidery floss**

X **Hand-sewing needle and thread**

X **Freezer paper**

Seam allowances:
⅝ inch (1.6 cm) unless otherwise noted

Shown in size 8

Patch It Up

What You Do

Make the Dress and Appliqué

1 Make the dress according to the basic instructions (page 30).

2 Use the petal template to cut two petals from each of the six petal fabrics. (Depending on the size of the dress you're making, you may want to alter the enlargement percentage.)

3 Arrange the fabric petals edge to edge in a pleasing sequence to form a circle with a hole in the center. Sew two petals along one straight side with the right sides together. Continue until you've joined all the petals and the circle is complete. Press the petal seams to the right.

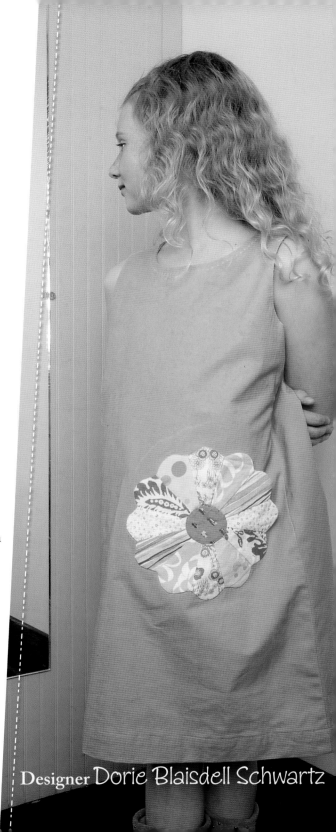

Designer Dorie Blaisdell Schwartz

4 Pin the circle of petals to the pocket lining with the right sides together. Sew around the outside of the circle of petals. Clip the curves, right up to—but not into—the stitching line at each V where the petals come together. Turn the pocket right side out by pulling it through the hole in the center of the flower. Use a pencil or a chopstick to make sure the curves at the end of each petal are neat. Press the pocket.

5 Cut 1 flower center from the freezer paper and the orange fabric using the template. Refer to the ladder-stitch appliqué technique on page 19 to make and attach the flower center to the center of the flower pocket. Figure 1 shows the extra ¼ inch (6mm) of the flower center fabric being pressed over the edge of the freezer paper.

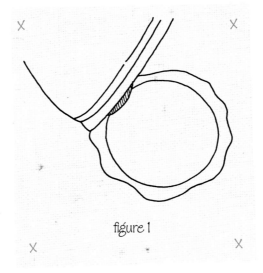

figure 1

6 Pin the flower pocket to the right hip of the dress so the top of the flower is at the waistline and the side of the flower is 1 inch (2.5 cm) from the side seam. Adjust the placement depending on the size of the dress. Sew the pocket to the dress using the ladder stitch (page 19). Leave the four petals toward the top and side seam (the place that would be north-west if the flower were a compass) unstitched so the pocket is accessible to little hands!

7 For an extra touch, embroider the neckline with a running stitch (page 22) ⅜ inch (1 cm) from the top of the neckline using three strands of yellow embroidery floss. Now take it out for a twirl.

Refashion one of Daddy's old shirts into a new dress for his little girl. If he's not willing to part with one, your local thrift shops will have plenty to choose from.

What You Need

X **Basic Sewing Kit (page 11)**

X **Basic Pattern**

X **1 man's shirt, size Large**

Seam allowances:

⅝ inch (1.6 cm) unless otherwise noted

Shown in size 7

The Shirt Off Daddy's Back

What You Do

Alter the Pattern

1 The back and front facing pieces are not used to make this dress. The dress front pattern piece does not require any pattern alteration. On the dress back pattern piece, draw a new center back pattern line ⅝ inch (1.6 cm) in from the existing line and cut along this line. This eliminates the seam allowance, so you can cut the dress back on the fold of the fabric. The dress will open in the front with the existing shirt buttons.

Note

This technique works with any man's shirt. The sample shows a nice denim chambray—super soft because it's been worn for years. How about using a man's dress shirt with a pocket made from an old tie?

Make the Dress

1 Cut the shirt apart at the side seams so you can cut the front and back pattern pieces from the front and back of the shirt separately. If the shirt has a front pocket, pick out the stitches with a seam ripper and remove it, but save it in case you want to stitch it back onto the dress later. Save the sleeves to make bias binding strips.

2 Fold the front of the shirt in half so the buttons are along the fold. Position and pin the front pattern piece so that the center fold line is along the fold of the shirt and the bottom of the dress pattern is lined up approximately with the bottom of the shirt. (If you use the existing shirt bottom, then you don't have to hem the finished dress.) Cut out the dress front.

3 Fold the back of the shirt in half; if there is a pleat, fold it in half. Position and pin the back pattern piece so that the center back fold is along the fold of the shirt and the bottom of the dress pattern is lined up with the bottom of the shirt, as you did for the dress front. Cut out the dress back.

4 Sew the front to the back at the shoulders, with the right sides of the shirt together. Press the seam allowances toward the back. If there is a back yoke on the shirt, treat it as one with the back of the dress.

5 For an enclosed seam finish, trim only the back seam allowance to about ¼ inch (6 mm).

6 Fold the wider, front seam allowance so it wraps around the raw edge of the back seam allowance (figure 1).

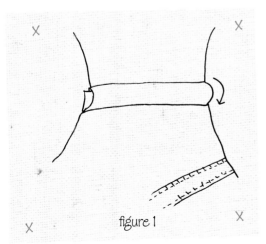

figure 1

Designer Wendi Gratz

7 Stitch close to the folded edge (figure 2).

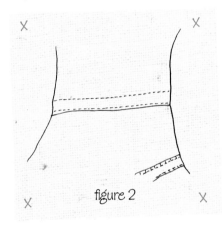

figure 2

8 Stitch the side seams. Press the seam allowances toward the back and finish them the same as the shoulder seams in steps 5 through 7.

9 Using extra fabric from the sleeves, cut bias strips 1⅝ inches (4.1 cm) wide and more than long enough to cover the raw edges at the neck and around the arms (page 25). Join strips if necessary.

10 Press one long edge of the bias strip ½ inch (1.3 cm) to the wrong side. With the raw edges and right sides together, pin the bias strip to the neck edge of the dress, folding each short edge ½ inch (1.3 cm) to the wrong side (figure 3).

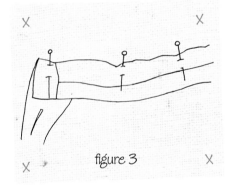

figure 3

11 Stitch the binding to the neck edge. Trim the seam allowance to ¼ inch (6 mm). Fold the bias strip to the inside of the dress to enclose the seam allowances and stitch close to the pressed fold.

12 Repeat steps 10 and 11 to bind both armholes.

13 If you want, replace the pocket. If the fabric around the original pocket location is bleached out, you'll probably want to cover that. If the pocket didn't leave any trace of itself on the shirt, then you can put it anywhere. Go show Daddy how great his old shirt looks now.

Sometimes it's the little touches that transform a basic dress. This is definitely a dress for special occasions; the fabric is lush dupioni silk and the beaded trim at the hem makes it extra fancy.

What You Need

- X **Basic Sewing Kit (page 11)**
- X **Basic Pattern**
- X **Fabric (Refer to Yardage Chart for Basic Dress on page 30)**
- X **1 button**
- X **1½ yards (1.4 m) of beaded trim**
- X **Zipper presser foot**

Seam allowances:
  ⅝ inch (1.6 cm) unless otherwise noted

Shown in size 7

Beadazzling

What You Do

Make the Dress

1 Make the dress according to the basic instructions (page 30).

2 Cut a piece of trim equal to the hem circumference plus 1 inch (2.5 cm). Knot the threads at the cut to prevent the beads from falling off. Fold the ends ½ inch (1.3 cm) to the wrong side. Pin the trim to the bottom edge of the right side of the dress so that the ends meet or overlap slightly in the center back or at a side seam. The beads will hang below the bottom edge of the dress.

3 Topstitch the trim in place along both the top and the bottom edges of the band. If the beads are large, use a zipper foot so you can stitch as close as possible to the edge of the trim.

Tip

Silk dupioni, the fabric I used for this dress, isn't machine washable, so I didn't worry about whether the trim was washable either. If you're working with a fabric that's machine washable, apply the trim with snap tape instead of stitching it down permanently. Attach one side of the snap tape to the trim and the other inside the bottom edge of the hem so you can remove the embellishment before washing.

Designer Wendi Gratz

Getting Ruffled

If you hate to hem, merrily skip that dreaded step and add a pretty ruffle in a contrasting color instead. It's a frilly embellishment that makes a simple dress simply wonderful.

What You Need

X **Basic Sewing Kit (page 11)**

X **Basic Pattern**

X **Fabric (Refer to Yardage Chart for Basic Dress on page 30)**

X **⅓ yard (30.5 cm) of fabric for the ruffle**

X **1 button**

X **Zipper foot**

Seam allowances:

⅝ inch (1.6 cm) unless otherwise noted

Shown in size 5

What You Do

Make the Dress

1 Make the dress according to the basic instructions (page 30). Skip step 15, the hemming of the dress.

2 Measure around the bottom of the dress (an approximate measurement is fine). Multiply that measurement by two to determine the cutting length for the ruffle. The cutting width is 5 inches (12.7 cm) for a 2-inch-wide (5.1 cm) ruffle. Cut out the ruffle according to these measurements; if the fabric isn't wide enough to cut it in one piece, cut two pieces and join them to get the length you need.

3 Stitch the short ends of the ruffle with the right sides together so you have one big circle. Fold the ruffle in half widthwise, with the wrong sides together, to make a circle of fabric that looks pretty from both sides, and press.

4 Set your machine to the longest stitch possible. Sew a row of basting stitches all the way around the loop, ¼ inch (6 mm) from the raw edges. Sew a second row halfway between the first row and the raw edge. Do not backstitch; instead, leave long thread tails at the beginning and end of the stitching.

Tip

A second row of basting stitches seems like one of those silly home ec rules, but whenever I try to take a shortcut and sew just one row of gathering stitches my thread always breaks and I have to start all over again. I've never had the thread break when I sew a double row.

5 Wrap the basting threads at one end around a straight pin so they don't pull out. Gently pull the other basting threads and watch the fabric gather into beautiful little folds. Keep pulling the threads until the fabric ruffle is the same length as the bottom of the dress.

6 Pin the ruffle to the right side of the bottom of the dress, with the raw edges of the ruffle lined up at the bottom of the dress. Don't sew anything yet! You have several raw edges here, so we're going to do a fancy little trick to finish this seam. Cut a strip of dress or ruffle fabric 2¼ inches (5.7 cm) wide and long enough to go around the bottom of the dress, plus 3 inches (7.6 cm).

Tip

For a novelty finish, use contrast fabric for the finishing strip. Sew the ruffle to the wrong side of the dress (so the raw edges are on the outside). This way, when you sew and turn up the finishing strip you'll have an extra snazzy strip between the ruffle and the dress. Extra embellishment with no extra effort!

7 Press the finishing strip in half lengthwise with wrong sides together. Pin the strip to the right side of the bottom of the dress (starting and ending near the center back), with the ruffle between the dress and the strip and the raw edges aligned (figure 1).

8 Sew the layers together with a ½-inch-wide (1.3 cm) seam, starting and stopping 2 or 3 inches (5.1 or 7.6 cm) before the beginning and end of the finishing strip. When the stitching nears the beginning of the seam, fold about 1 inch (2.5 cm) of the finishing strip back on itself (figure 2). Trim off any extra length.

9 Lay the opposite end of the finishing strip over this fold so it overlaps by about 1 inch (2.5 cm). Trim off any extra length. Continue stitching to finish the seam; backstitch. Trim the seam allowance to ⅛ inch (3 mm).

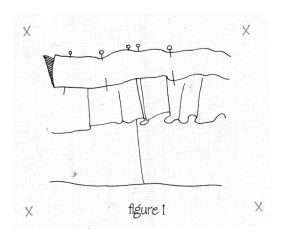

figure 1

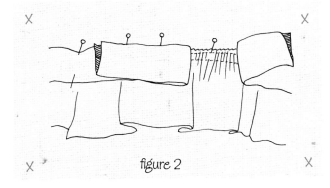

figure 2

Note

You can use this finishing technique for lots of other projects. It's easy to add a custom ruffle to the bottom of almost any purchased garment. It works great on dresses, pants, shirts, jackets, sleeves, etc. And the ruffle isn't just for decoration! If your child (like mine) grows up and not out, you can use ruffles to extend the length of too-short dresses or pants. For best results, pick open or cut off the existing hem; otherwise, the seam gets very bulky.

10 Press the finishing strip with the nice, clean, folded edge to the inside, encasing the raggedy edges (figure 3). Stitch close to the folded edge. There's a lot of fabric in there—I used a zipper foot so the bulk didn't push me off my stitching line.

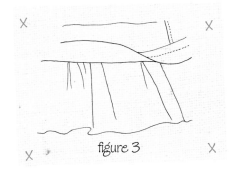

figure 3

A drawstring waist completely changes the silhouette of the simple A-line. White eyelet is the perfect fabric for little girls on a summer day.

What You Need

- ✗ Basic Sewing Kit (page 11)
- ✗ Basic Pattern
- ✗ Fabric (Refer to the chart on page 65)
- ✗ 1 button
- ✗ 1 yard (0.9 m) of 1½-inch-wide (3.8 cm) grosgrain ribbon
- ✗ 2 yards (1.8 m) of satin cord
- ✗ Disappearing-ink fabric marker

Seam allowances:
⅝ inch (1.6 cm) unless otherwise noted

Shown in size 4

Summer Sweetness

What You Do

Make the Dress

1 Cut the dress front and back pattern pieces in both the eyelet and the lining fabrics. The lining pieces replace the facings, so don't cut the facings. Cut 1 inch (2.5 cm) off the bottom of the front and back lining pieces.

2 Sew the dress following the basic instructions on page 30, substituting the lining pieces for the facings. Hem the lining and the eyelet dress separately, so the lining is shorter than the outer dress.

3 Try the dress on the child and pin or mark the waistline with the fabric marker. Pin the ribbon on the outer (eyelet) dress at the marked waistline. Fold the short, cut edges of the ribbon to the wrong side so they abut at the center back. Stitch the ribbon onto the eyelet dress (pin or move the lining out of the way of the stitching) close to both long edges so it forms a casing for the drawstring.

Designer Wendi Gratz

4 Cut the satin cord to the desired length, knot one end, and thread the unknotted end through the casing. (Attach a safety pin to the unknotted end if you need help getting the cording through the casing.) Once the cording is through the casing, knot the other end. After the dress is on, pull the cording to create the desired silhouette. Warning: Every little girl's white dress is fated to get smeared with chocolate ice cream, but put it on her anyway because white eyelet is just so pretty.

	SIZE 3	SIZE 4	SIZE 5	SIZE 6	SIZE 7	SIZE 8
MAIN FABRIC	¾ yd (68.6 cm)	1 yd (0.9 m)	1 yd (0.9 m)	1 yd (0.9 m)	1 yd (0.9 m)	1 yd (0.9 m)
LINING	¾ yd (68.6 cm)	1 yd (0.9 m)	1 yd (0.9 m)	1 yd (0.9 m)	1 yd (0.9 m)	1 yd (0.9 m)

Yardage is the same for all fabric widths.

Designer Wendi Gratz

Borderlines

Forget about facings and finish the garment edges with bias trim instead. Normally you'd fold bias trim to the inside of the dress, but for this project I used contrasting colors and stitched the colorful bands to the outside to create sassy borders.

What You Need

- X **Basic Sewing Kit (page 11)**
- X **Basic Pattern**
- X **Fabric (Refer to the chart at right)**
- X **4 contrasting fabric remnants for bias trim**
- X **12- to 14-inch (30.5 to 35.6 cm) zipper**
- X **Zipper presser foot**

Seam allowances:
  ⅝ inch (1.6 cm) unless otherwise noted

Shown in size 6

What You Do

Make the Dress

1 Cut out the dress front and dress back, but don't cut out the facings.

2 Cut bias strips of fabric 1⅝ inches (4.8 cm) wide from four different color fabrics (page 25). Sew strips together as needed so each colored strip is long enough to go around the armholes, neck, or the hem of the dress.

3 Install the zipper presser foot on your sewing machine and insert the zipper in the center back seam, according to the instructions on page 26.

4 Sew the front to the back at the shoulders with the right sides together. Press the seams toward the back.

5 Sew the front to the back at the sides with the right sides together. Press the seams toward the back.

6 Press ¾ inch (1.3 cm) to the wrong side along the length of one side of each of the bias binding strips.

7 Pin an armhole bias strip to one armhole with the right side of the strip facing the wrong side of the dress and raw edges aligned. Overlap the binding strip ends slightly. Stitch the bias strip to the dress with a ⅝-inch (1.6 cm) seam allowance. Trim and clip the seam allowance.

8 Turn the folded edge of the bias strip to the right side of the dress. Stitch the bias strip in place as close as possible to the folded edge, and press.

9 Repeat for the second armhole and the hem.

10 Pin the neckline bias strip in place so it extends ⅝ inch (1.6 cm) beyond the center back seam of the dress on each side, just above the zipper. Stitch the bias tape as you did in step 7.

11 At the zipper, fold the extended bias tape ends inside the dress and catch them in the finishing stitching. Proceed as in step 8.

	SIZE 3	SIZE 4	SIZE 5	SIZE 6	SIZE 7	SIZE 8
MAIN FABRIC	¾ yd (68.6 cm)	1 yd (0.9 m)	1 yd (0.9 m)	1 yd (0.9 m)	1 yd (0.9 m)	1 yd (0.9 m)
Yardage is the same for all fabric widths.						

Designer Wendi Gratz

Not only are wrap dresses cute, but they're easy for even the littlest girls to put on and take off themselves— no hard-to-reach back zippers or buttons. Let the fun begin!

What You Need

X **Basic Sewing Kit (page 11)**

X **Basic Pattern**

X **Fabric (Refer to the chart on page 70)**

X **Large piece of paper, twice the size as the pattern front piece**

X **2 buttons**

X **Pencil**

X **Ruler or yardstick**

X **Hand-sewing needle and thread**

Seam allowances:

  ⅝ **inch (1.6 cm) unless otherwise noted**

Shown in size 3

Wrap-a-Rama

What You Do

Alter the Pattern

1 Fold the paper in half. Lay the dress front pattern piece so the fold line on the pattern aligns with the fold of the paper. Trace the pattern piece onto the paper. Cut it out and unfold it so you have a new pattern piece for the full front of the dress.

2 Refold the new pattern piece in half. Measure down approximately 1 inch (2.5 cm) from the bottom of the armhole and make a mark. Draw a gently curving line connecting the center front at the neckline to the mark under the armhole. It should look like a natural continuation of the original half of the neckline curve. Cut away the top piece of the paper along the drawn line; it's shown folded in half here (figure 1).

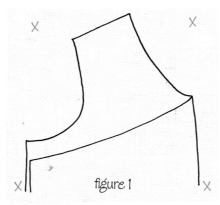

figure 1

3 Unfold the new dress front pattern piece. You will now cut two dress fronts using this full front pattern (figure 2).

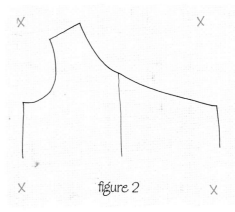

figure 2

4 Since the back of the dress no longer needs an opening, cut away the ⅝-inch (1.6 cm) seam allowance at the center back seam on the dress back pattern piece.

Cut the Fabric

1 Cut out two dress fronts and one dress back from both the dress and the lining fabrics, being sure to cut out the dress back with the new center back marking on the fold of the fabrics. Do not cut any facings.

Make the Dress

1 Staystitch (page 18) the curved front and back neck edges, ½ inch (1.3 cm) from the cut edge. Stitch the front of the dress to the back at the shoulder seams with the right sides together. Press the seams open. Repeat with the front and back lining pieces.

2 Pin the dress to the lining with right sides together at the neck edges and armhole edges. Stitch the seams, trim the seam allowances, and clip the curves.

3 Turn the dress right side out by pulling each front piece through the shoulders. Press the neck and armhole seams.

4 Stitch the side seams as in steps 9 and 10 of the basic instructions, treating the lining as the facings. Take care to keep the wrap, or extended edge, of each front piece out of the side seam.

5 Turn the dress inside out enough to sew the dress to the lining at the front edges and the bottom with the right sides of the fabrics together. Leave between 4 and 6 inches (10.2 and 15.2 cm) unstitched along one of the front edges. Pull the dress through this opening to turn it right side out. Press all the edges. Hand stitch the opening closed using the ladder stitch (page 19).

6 Try the dress on the child and wrap it as desired. Mark the button placement under each armhole, just in front of the side seam.

7 Stitch buttonholes according to your machine instructions, or as on page 28, and hand sew the buttons in place. Ready for some sushi?

	SIZE 3	SIZE 4	SIZE 5	SIZE 6	SIZE 7	SIZE 8
DRESS FABRIC	1½ yd (1.4 m)	1½ yd (1.4 m)	1½ yd (1.4 m)	1¾ yd (1.6 m)	1¾ yd (1.6 m)	2 yd (1.8 m)
LINING	1½ yd (1.4 m)	1½ yd (1.4 m)	1½ yd (1.4 m)	1¾ yd (1.6 m)	1¾ yd (1.6 m)	2 yd (1.8 m)
	Yardage is the same for all fabric widths.					

Tip
Make sure the dress and lining fabrics are similar weights.

Aren't reversible clothes fun? Squares one day, circles the next. Give your favorite girl some nifty fabrics to switch to her heart's content; she may want to reverse them half-way through the day!

Designer Wendi Gratz

What You Need

X **Basic Sewing Kit (page 11)**

X **Basic Pattern**

X **Fabric (Refer to the chart at right)**

X **1 hook-and-eye closure**

X **Hand-sewing needle and thread**

Seam allowances:
⅝ inch (1.6 cm) unless otherwise noted

Shown in size 6

Double Duty

What You Do

Make the Dress

1 Cut the dress front and back pieces from both fabrics. Do not cut the facing pieces. Staystitch (page 18) the curved front and back neck edges, ½ inch (1.3 cm) from the cut edge.

2 Pin and sew the front and back pieces of fabric A with right sides together at the shoulders. Repeat with fabric B. The fabric B dress replaces the facings, so with right sides together, sew the two dresses together at the neck and armholes, following the instructions on page 31, steps 6 through 13. When the instructions refer to the facings, substitute fabric B dress.

3 Pin the raw edges of the lower center back seam of dress B with wrong sides together and stitch from the large dot to the bottom of the dress. Backstitch and press the seam open.

	SIZE 3	SIZE 4	SIZE 5	SIZE 6	SIZE 7	SIZE 8
FABRIC A	**45" (1.1 m) wide** 1 yd (0.9 m)	$1\frac{1}{8}$ yd (1 m)	$1\frac{1}{8}$ yd (1 m)	$1\frac{1}{4}$ yd (1.1 m)	$1\frac{1}{2}$ yd (1.4 m)	$1\frac{3}{4}$ yd (1.6 m)
	60" (1.5 m) wide $\frac{7}{8}$ yd (80 cm)	$\frac{7}{8}$ yd (180 cm)	1 yd (0.9 m)	1 yd (0.9 m)	1 yd (0.9 m)	$1\frac{1}{8}$ yd (0.9 m)
FABRIC B	**45" (1.1 m) wide** 1 yd (0.9 m)	$1\frac{1}{8}$ yd (1 m)	$1\frac{1}{8}$ yd (1 m)	$1\frac{1}{4}$ yd (1.1 m)	$1\frac{1}{2}$ yd (1.4 m)	$1\frac{3}{4}$ yd (1.6 m)
	60" (1.5 m) wide $\frac{7}{8}$ yd (80 cm)	$\frac{7}{8}$ yd (180 cm)	1 yd (0.9 m)	1 yd (0.9 m)	1 yd (0.9 m)	$1\frac{1}{8}$ yd (0.9 m)

4 Try the dress on the child and mark the desired hem length. Cut both fabrics 1 inch (2.5 cm) longer than the marked length. Hem the fabrics together as one. Decide which fabric will have a contrast hem band and fold the bottom of both fabrics under ½ inch (1.3 cm) and then under ½ inch (1.3 cm) again toward that side. Stitch close to the folded edge and press.

5 Hand stitch a hook-and-eye closure to the top of the back opening; it works well whichever way the dress is turned. So, which fabric do you want facing out to start with?

Tip
Make sure to use two fabrics of similar weights.

This swishy dress is extra special and extra fun to wear because it has two layers. Beautiful sheer fabrics aren't tricky to use—you just have to line them with a less-sheer fabric.

What You Need

X **Basic Sewing Kit (page 11)**

X **Basic Pattern**

X **Fabric (Refer to the chart on page 76)**

X **1 button**

Seam allowances:

⅝ inch (1.6 cm) unless otherwise noted

Shown in size 5

Sheer Genius

What You Do

Make the Dress

1 Cut the dress front and back pieces in both sheer and lining fabrics. The lining replaces the facings, so don't cut facing pieces.

2 Sew the dress following the basic instructions on page 30, substituting the lining pieces for the facings.

3 Narrow hem or serge hem the sheer dress and the lining separately.

Note

You don't have to stop at two layers. My mother-in-law made a lovely dress for my daughter out of four layers of sheer fabrics, with each layer 1 or 2 inches (2.5 or 5.1 cm) shorter than the layer beneath it. If you use enough layers of sheer fabrics you don't have to worry about an opaque lining and the dress will have a beautiful floatiness.

Designer Wendi Gratz

Tip

Sheer fabrics can be fussy to hem. You don't want to use the normal ½-inch (1.3 cm) hem because it will be visible through the sheer fabric and might look heavy. I like to serge the bottom edge for a nice clean look—but don't despair if you don't own a serger. Here is a trick for stitching a narrow hem on sheer fabric.

Apply spray starch liberally along the bottom of the dress to help it hold a pressed edge. Machine sew ¼ inch (6 mm) from the hem edge to create a turning guideline. Fold and press the fabric to the wrong side along the stitching line. Turn it under another ¼ inch (6 mm) and press again. Machine stitch close to the pressed edge. The bottom of the dress will look stiff and weird at first, but the starch will come out in the wash and you'll have a beautiful finished edge.

	SIZE 3	SIZE 4	SIZE 5	SIZE 6	SIZE 7	SIZE 8
MAIN FABRIC	¾ yd (68.6 cm)	1 yd (0.9 m)	1 yd (0.9 m)	1 yd (0.9 m)	1 yd (0.9 m)	1 yd (0.9 m)
LINING	¾ yd (68.6 cm)	1 yd (0.9 m)	1 yd (0.9 m)	1 yd (0.9 m)	1 yd (0.9 m)	1 yd (0.9 m)

Yardage is the same for all fabric widths.

Adding More

Diamonds may be a girl's best friend, but it's rhinestones that take center stage on this absolutely fabulous dress. It promises to be a favorite for little girls everywhere.

What You Need

- X **Basic Sewing Kit (page 11)**
- X **Basic Pattern**
- X **Collar Template (page 127)**
- X **Fabric (Refer to Yardage Chart for Basic Dress on page 30)**
- X **¾ yard (68.6 cm) of collar fabric**
- X **¾ yard (68.6 cm) of fusible interfacing**
- X **1 hook-and-eye closure**
- X **Assorted rhinestone crystal jewels (use less for smaller sizes):**
  - X **20 round 18 mm rhinestones**
  - X **15 round 15 mm rhinestones**
  - X **100 round 7 mm rhinestones**
  - X **22 oval 15 x 7 mm rhinestones**
  - X **15 triangle 12 mm rhinestones**
- X **Fabric adhesive**
- X **Toothpicks**

Seam allowances:
⅝ inch (1.6 cm) unless otherwise noted

Shown in size 8

Bling It On

What You Do

Make the Collar

1 Using the collar template, cut two collar front pieces and four collar back pieces from the chosen collar fabric. Cut one collar front piece and two collar back pieces from interfacing, using the same pattern.

2 Fuse the interfacing to the wrong side of one of the front collars and two of the back collars, following the manufacturer's instructions.

3 With the right sides together, stitch the interfaced collar front and collar back pieces together at the shoulders. Repeat with the non-interfaced pieces. Carefully press the seams open.

4 Pin the interfaced and non-interfaced collars with the right sides together. Stitch them together along each back (the short, straight edges) and the outside curve. Leave the inside curve unstitched. Trim the seam allowances and clip the curves. Turn the collar right side out and press. Set the collar aside.

Make the Dress

1 Make the dress following steps 1 through 5 in the basic instructions (page 30).

2 Before sewing the facing to the dress (step 6 of the basic instructions), pin the collar to the neck of the dress. Baste the collar in place (figure 1).

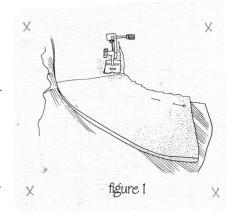

figure 1

Designer Joan K. Morris

79

3 Continue with the basic instructions for steps 6 through 15 (page 31), catching the collar in the stitching between the dress and the facings.

4 To help the collar lay flat, lift it away from the dress and stitch ½ inch (1.3 cm) below the collar seam on the dress fabric, catching the seam allowance in the stitching (figure 2).

5 Substitute the button and wrapped thread loop closure with the simpler (and nearly invisible) hook-and-eye closure, following the instructions on the package.

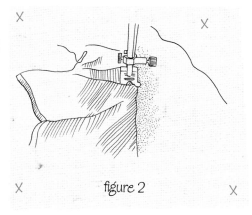

figure 2

Bring the Bling

1 Lay the dress flat with the collar extended. Arrange the jewels on the collar any way you like. I recommend that you start with the large jewels and fill in with the smaller ones. It's easier to match sides if you start placing jewels in the center and work your way out.

2 Once you're pleased with the arrangement, apply adhesive to the back of the jewels with toothpicks, following the manufacturer's instructions. Set up a red carpet event in your neighborhood—this dress is worthy of nothing less.

Designer Rebeka Lambert

Butterfly Wings

Adding sleeves is easy. Your little butterfly will especially love these pretty flutter sleeves.

What You Need

- X **Basic Sewing Kit (page 11)**
- X **Basic Pattern**
- X **Fabric (Refer to the chart at right)**
- X **Large piece of paper**
- X **1 button**
- X **Measuring tape**
- X **Dressmaker's curved ruler**

Seam allowances:

⅝ inch (1.6 cm) unless otherwise noted

Shown in size 3

What You Do

Alter the Dress Pattern

1 Trace the dress front and back pattern pieces onto paper. Mark a line 3½ inches (8.9 cm) up from and parallel to the lower edge (figure 1).

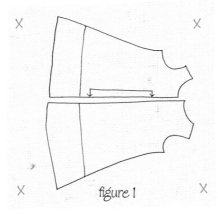

figure 1

2 Cut the pattern pieces apart along the marked line to make a total of four pieces—dress front, band front, dress back, and band back. Add ¼-inch (6 mm) seam allowances along the bottom of the dress pieces and the top of the band pieces.

3 Cut out the dress front, dress back, and facings from your main fabric. Cut out the bottom bands from the coordinating fabric.

Make the Flutter Sleeves

1 The flutter sleeve is a semicircular piece of fabric that is sewn to the top half of the armhole. Making the pattern for it isn't an exact science, so your measurements don't have to be perfect. Look at the armhole curves on the front and back of the dress patterns and make a mark just above the middle of the armhole curves. The flutter sleeve will be stitched between these two markings.

	SIZE 3	SIZE 4	SIZE 5	SIZE 6	SIZE 7	SIZE 8
MAIN FABRIC	**45" (1.1 m) wide** 1 yd (0.9 m)	1⅛ yd (1 m)	1⅛ yd (1 m)	1¼ yd (1.1 m)	1½ yd (1.4 m)	1¾ yd (1.6 m)
	60" (1.5 m) wide ⅞ yd (80 cm)	⅞ yd (80 cm)	1 yd (0.9 m)	1 yd (0.9 m)	1 yd (0.9 m)	1⅛ yd (1 m)
SLEEVES/ HEM BAND FABRIC	¼ yd (22.9 cm)	¼ yd (22.9 cm)	¼ yd (22.9 cm)	½ yd (45.7 cm)	½ yd (45.7 cm)	½ yd (45.7 cm)

For the sleeves/hem band fabric, yardage is the same for all fabric widths.

2 Position the front and back dress pattern pieces together at the shoulder. Measure the pattern along the armhole between the markings and double that measurement. This will be the length of the top curve of the sleeve; the depth of the sleeve is about 3 inches (7.6 cm), as shown in figure 2. Follow the illustration to make the sleeve pattern, and use the dressmaker's curved ruler to draw an evenly shaped pattern piece. Use the pattern to cut four sleeves from the contrasting fabric.

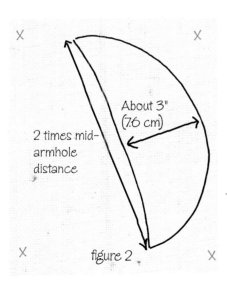

2 times mid-armhole distance

About 3" (7.6 cm)

figure 2

3 Pin two sleeve pieces with the right sides together and stitch along the straight edge. Turn the sleeve right side out and press. Run two rows of gathering stitches along the curved edge. Use a pin to mark the center of the curved edge. Repeat with the remaining sleeve pieces.

Make the Dress

1 Pin the bottom bands to the front and back dress pieces with right sides together. Stitch the seams with ¼-inch (6 mm) seam allowances. Press the seams open.

2 Assemble the dress following the basic instructions steps 2 through 5 (page 30). Sew the dress and the neck facings together at the neck edge, but don't sew the armhole facings to the dress yet.

Note

You can make the flutter sleeves from almost any fabric. Try using a really fancy fabric like glittery organza. Experiment with the size of the flutter sleeve, too—stiff fabric allows you to make the sleeve wider without worrying about it flopping over.

3 Pin one flutter sleeve to one armhole, matching the center of the sleeve with the shoulder seam of the dress and the ends of the sleeve with the markings; adjust the gathers as needed. Baste the sleeve in place (figure 3). Repeat with the remaining sleeve and armhole.

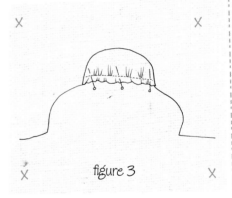

figure 3

4 Pin the dress and armhole facings with the right sides together and the sleeves sandwiched between them; stitch the armhole seams. Trim the seam allowances to roughly ¼ inch (6 mm) wide and clip the curves.

5 Follow the basic instructions from steps 7 through 16 to finish the dress (page 31).

In this outfit, your little sweetheart will be the best-dressed kid at the party—or on the playground!

What You Need

X **Basic Sewing Kit (page 11)**

X **Basic Pattern**

X **Placket Template (page 126)**

X **Fabric (Refer to Yardage Chart for Basic Dress on page 30)**

X ½ yard (45.7 cm) of white cotton fabric

X ½ yard (45.7 cm) of satin fabric

X 3 covered button blanks, ¾ inch (9.5 cm) in diameter

X 1 hook-and-eye closure

X Hem gauge

X Zipper foot

X Hand-sewing needle and thread

Seam allowances:
5/8 inch (1.6 cm) unless otherwise noted

Shown in size 6

Puttin' on the Ritz

What You Do

Make the Pleated Placket

1 Cut a piece of the white cotton fabric 16 x 22 inches (40.6 x 55.9 cm). Fold it in half so that it's 16 x 11 inches (40.6 x 27.9 cm). Press the fold to mark the center and open it back up.

2 Measure and mark ¾ inch (1.9 cm) from each side of the pressed center fold. Fold and press the fabric along the markings so ½ inch (1.3 cm) of fabric is folded under the pleat on each side to create the center 1½-inch-wide (3.8 cm) pleat.

3 Pleat the fabric toward each outside edge, one side at a time. Measure and mark ½-inch (1.3 cm) pleats (figure 1); fold and press the pleats until you have at least three additional pleats on each side of the center pleat.

4 Place the placket template on top of the pleated fabric so the center line of the template is directly over the middle of the center pleat. To adjust for the size of your dress, you may want to add additional pleats (or perhaps remove some); leave at least 1 inch (2.5 cm) of unpleated fabric at each side. When you're happy with the amount of pleating you have, pin the template in place and cut out the placket. Baste around the edges to hold the pleats in place (figure 2).

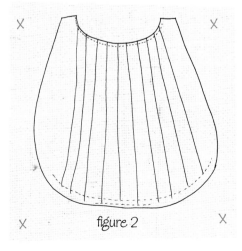

figure 2

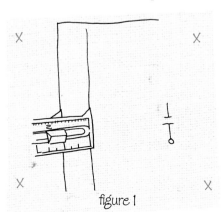

figure 1

5 Using the same template and the rest of your white fabric, cut out a second (unpleated) placket piece.

6 Pin the pleated and unpleated placket pieces right sides together and stitch around the edge with a ½-inch (1.3 cm) seam allowance. Leave the top neck edge open. Trim the seams and clip the curves. Turn the placket right side out and press it flat.

Make the Dress

1 Make the dress according to the basic instructions, steps 1 and 2 (page 30).

2 Cut a piece of the satin 4½ x 42 inches (11.4 x 106.7 cm). Fold this piece in half the long way, with wrong sides together, and press.

3 Baste two rows of stitching, ⅛ inch (3 mm) apart, along the raw edges. Don't backstitch; instead, leave the thread tails long. Pull the threads to gather the fabric so that it fits around the sides and bottom of the placket. Distribute the gathers evenly.

Note

This dress doesn't have to be made up in black, white, and satin. For a more casual look, make it in fun cotton prints.

Designer Joan K. Morris

4 Pin the flat side of the placket to the right side of the dress front so that the neck edges align. Baste the necklines together.

5 Pin the gathered ruffle around the sides and lower edge of the placket so that the raw edges are ½ inch (1.3 cm) under the edge of the placket. Smooth and distribute the gathers evenly as you pin (figure 3). Baste the ruffle to the dress at the shoulders.

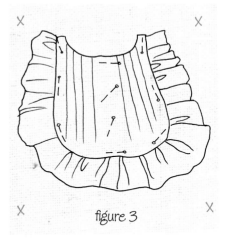

figure 3

6 Edgestitch (page 18) the placket and ruffle to the dress as close as possible to the edge of the placket.

7 Follow steps 3 through 14 of the basic instructions (page 30).

Hem the Dress

1 Try the dress on the child and mark the desired hem length. Make a second marking 2 inches (5.1 cm) above the desired hem length to allow for a 2½-inch-wide (6.4 cm) ruffle and ½-inch (1.3 cm) seam allowance. Cut away the extra fabric below the second marking.

2 Cut a piece of satin 6 x 60 inches (15.2 cm x 1.5 m). (If necessary, join two pieces to obtain the right length.)

3 Stitch the short ends of the ruffle with the right sides together so you have one big circle. Fold the ruffle in half widthwise, with the wrong sides together, to make a circle of fabric that looks pretty from both sides, and press.

4 Baste two rows of stitching, ⅛ inch (3 mm) apart, along the seam edge. Don't backstitch, and leave the thread tails long. Pull the threads to gather the fabric so that it fits around the hem of the dress. Distribute the gathers evenly.

5 Pin the ruffle to the right side of the bottom of the dress, with the raw edges of the ruffle lined up at the bottom of the dress. Cut a strip of dress or ruffle fabric 2¼ inches (5.7 cm) wide and long enough to go around the bottom of the dress, plus 3 inches (7.6 cm).

6 Press the finishing strip in half lengthwise with wrong sides together. Pin the strip to the right side of the bottom of the dress (starting and ending near the center back), with the ruffle between the dress and the strip and the raw edges aligned.

7 Sew the layers together with a ½-inch-wide (1.3 cm) seam, starting and stopping 2 or 3 inches (5.1 or 7.6 cm) before the beginning and end of the finishing strip. When the stitching nears the beginning of the seam, fold about 1 inch (2.5 cm) of the finishing strip back on itself. Trim off any extra length.

8 Lay the opposite end of the finishing strip over this fold so it overlaps by about 1 inch (2.5 cm). Trim off any extra length. Continue stitching to finish the seam; backstitch. Trim the seam allowance to ⅛ inch (3 mm).

9 Press the finishing strip with the nice, clean, folded edge to the inside, encasing the raggedy edges. Stitch close to the folded edge. There's a lot of fabric in there. Use a zipper foot so the bulk doesn't push you off the stitching line.

Finish the Dress

1 Following the manufacturer's instructions, cover the three buttons in satin and hand stitch them onto the front placket.

2 Hand stitch the hook-and-eye closure onto the back of the dress. This dress was made for parties so...party down!

Designer Wendi Gratz

Cutting Up

A cute swingy top is easy to adapt from the basic pattern. What might be hard is making this zany tribe of monkeys behave!

What You Need

X Basic Sewing Kit (page 11)

X Basic Pattern

X Fabric (Refer to the chart at right)

X 1 button

Seam allowances:
⅝ inch (1.6 cm) unless otherwise noted

Shown in size 5

Sea Monkey Swing

What You Do

Alter the Pattern

1 Alter the dress front and back patterns by measuring 8 inches (20.3 cm) below the marked waistline on the pattern; draw a new cutting line at this spot and trim away the pattern below.

Make the Top

1 Make the top according to the basic dress instructions on page 30. Call your little monkey over to try it on for size.

Note

You can apply any of the dress embellishments in this book to this design. A ruffled hem, cross-stitched border, tuxedo collar—they'd all look just as great on a top!

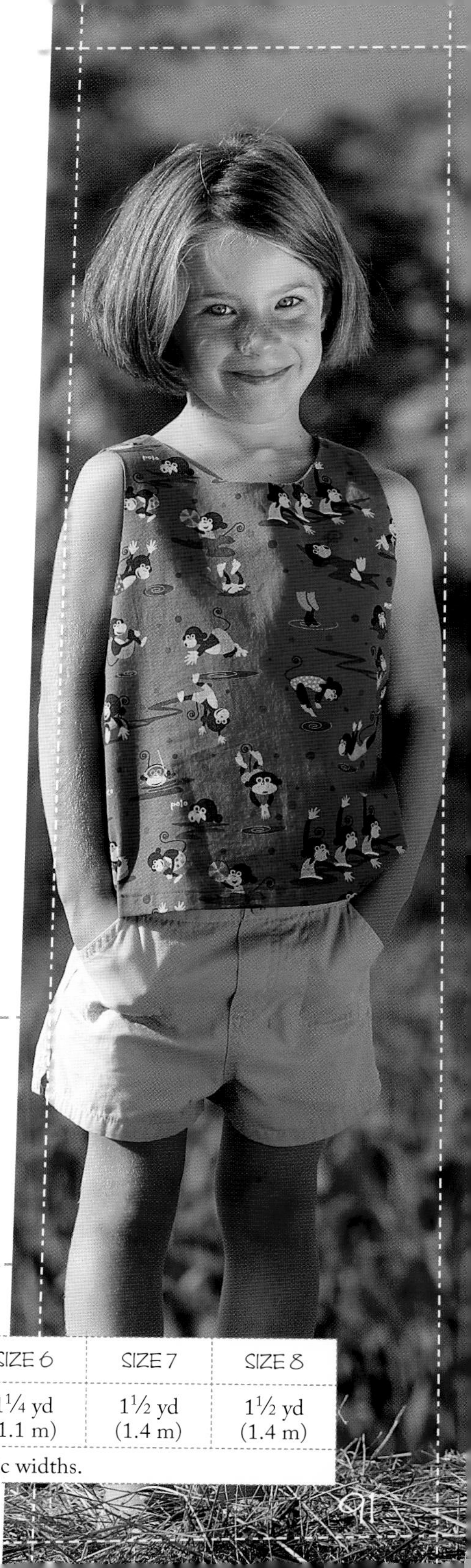

	SIZE 3	SIZE 4	SIZE 5	SIZE 6	SIZE 7	SIZE 8
MAIN FABRIC	¾ yd (68.6 cm)	1 yd (0.9 m)	1 yd (0.9 m)	1¼ yd (1.1 m)	1½ yd (1.4 m)	1½ yd (1.4 m)
Yardage is the same for all fabric widths.						

Who knew how easy it is to turn a dress into a skirt? And the elastic waist is a girl's best friend—practical and comfortable, too.

What You Need

X Basic Sewing Kit (page 11)

X Basic Pattern

X Fabric (Refer to the chart on page 95)

X Large piece of paper

X 1 yard (0.9 m) of single-fold bias tape for the waistband

X 1 yard (0.9 m) of elastic, ⅜ inch (1 cm) wide

X 2 yards (1.8 m) of double-fold bias tape for the contrasting hem

X Pencil

X Yardstick or ruler

X Safety pin

Seam allowances:
⅝ inch (1.6 cm) unless otherwise noted

Shown in size 6

Skirting the Issue

What You Do

Alter the Pattern and Cut the Fabric

1 At the marked waistline on the pattern, draw a straight line across the front dress pattern piece. Trace the new line and only the portion of the front dress below the line onto clean paper. This will be the only pattern piece you need.

2 Place the new pattern piece on the fold of the fabric and cut a skirt piece. Repeat to cut one more skirt piece, so you end up with two skirt pieces.

Designer Rebeka Lambert

Tip

You can always make your own bias binding to ensure a perfect color match (page 25).

Make the Skirt

1 Unfold both pieces and with the right sides together, sew the side seams. Turn the skirt right side out.

2 Press open the single-fold bias tape and align one edge with the top of the skirt. Stitch along the fold (figure 1), overlapping the ends.

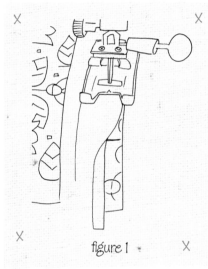

figure 1

3 Press the bias tape to the inside of the skirt. Stitch along the folded edge of the bias tape to create a casing for the elastic. Leave a 3-inch (7.6 cm) break in the stitching for inserting the elastic.

4 Cut a length of elastic that fits comfortably around the child's waist, plus 1 inch (2.5 cm). Using a safety pin, thread the elastic under the bias tape, through the opening in the stitching. Stitch the ends of the elastic together and then stitch the opening in the casing closed.

5 Encase the bottom edge of the skirt in double-fold bias tape: Pin the narrower side of the bias tape on the front of the skirt and the wider side on the back, overlapping the ends near one of the side seams. Edgestitch (page 18) along the fold of the bias tape to finish the lower edge.

	SIZE 3	SIZE 4	SIZE 5	SIZE 6	SIZE 7	SIZE 8
MAIN FABRIC	½ yd (45.7 cm)	½ yd (45.7 cm)	1 yd (0.9 m)	1 yd (0.9 m)	1¼ yd (1.1 m)	1½ yd (1.4 m)
Yardage is the same for all fabric widths.						

H.M.S. Pinafore

Girls young (and old) like to wear a pinafore over a pair of jeans—just to be pretty. Pick some cheerful fabrics for this clever adaptation of the basic dress.

What You Need

X **Basic Sewing Kit (page 11)**

X **Basic Pattern**

X **Fabric (Refer to Yardage Chart for Basic Dress on page 30)**

X **Fabric remnant, for the pockets**

X **Large piece of paper**

X **Hook-and-loop tape, remnant**

X **1 button**

Seam allowances:
⅝ inch (1.6 cm) unless otherwise noted

Shown in size 7

What You Do

Alter the Pattern

1 The front dress pattern is fine as it is. Do not use the facing pieces. Alter the back dress pattern piece on a large piece of paper as follows: draw a line from the top shoulder corner to the bottom edge, parallel to the center back. Draw a second line for the seam allowance, ⅝ inch (1.6 cm) from the first line as shown (figure 1). Cut the pattern along the second line.

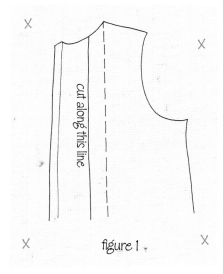

X

cut along this line

X

X   figure 1   X

Cut the Fabric

1 Cut two of the new back pieces and one front piece from the main fabric.

2 From the main fabric, cut two back belt pieces that are 6½ x 4½ inches (16.5 x 11.4 cm) large. Depending on the size of the dress you're making, you may want to alter these measurements a little. Also cut bias strips that are 1⅝ inches wide (4.1 cm) and long enough to go around both armholes, the neck opening, and down the back edges of both back pieces. This could take up to 9 yards (8.2 m), depending on the size of the dress. You will need to piece several lengths (page 25).

3 From the remnant fabric, cut four 5½-inch (14 cm) square pieces for the pockets.

Note

This pattern adaptation can be used to convert almost any dress in this book into a pinafore—make it as plain or as fancy as you like! You can even make a pinafore to coordinate with a dress.

Make the Pinafore

1 Sew the front to the back pieces at the shoulder seams and the side seams with the right sides together. Press the seam allowances toward the back.

2 Press one long edge of the bias strip ½ inch (1.3 cm) to the wrong side. With the right sides together and raw edges aligned, pin the bias strip to one of the armholes; stitch the seam. Trim and clip the seam allowance. Turn the folded edge of the bias strip to the inside of the armhole and stitch it in place. Repeat for the second armhole.

3 Fold one of the belt pieces with right sides together to form a rectangle 4½ x 3¼ inches (11.4 x 8.3 cm). Sew along one long and one short edge. Clip the corner, turn the belt right side out, and press (figure 2). Repeat with the second belt piece.

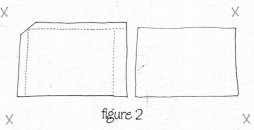

figure 2

4 Approximate the waist location on the back pieces. Pin the belt pieces at the waist so the raw edges of the belt line up with the raw edges of the pinafore (figure 3).

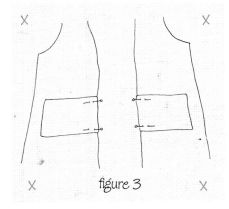

figure 3

5 Use the remaining bias strips to bind the neck and both back edges in one continuous seam. Pin the bias strip to the pinafore with right sides together and raw edges aligned, beginning at one bottom edge and continuing up one back edge, around the neck, and down the other back edge. Sandwich the pinned belt pieces between the bias strip and the pinafore.

6 Stitch the seam. Trim and clip the seam allowance. Turn the folded edge of the bias strip to the inside and stitch it in place. Press.

7 Sew a square of hook-and-loop tape to the top side of one belt flap and the underside of the other, or sew a button to one side and make a buttonhole on the other side.

8 Use a glass or a coffee cup as a guide to draw round bottoms on the pocket pieces. Cut along the markings.

9 Pin two of the pockets with right sides together. Using a ¼-inch (6 mm) seam allowance, sew around the edge, leaving a 2-inch (5.1 cm) opening along the bottom. Clip the corners and curves and turn the pocket right side out through the opening. Press the pocket, tucking the raw edges of the opening to the inside so the whole pocket looks finished. Repeat with the two remaining pocket pieces.

10 Pin the pockets on the front of the pinafore in the desired location. Edgestitch (page 18) the pockets onto the pinafore. Backstitch (page 18) at the beginning and end of the seam (do not stitch across the top of the pockets). This stitching will attach the pockets and close up the opening that was left for turning the pockets—no hand stitching necessary.

Jump Around

Go from A-line in summer to jumper in winter by using wool fabrics. The addition of an empire waist adds a snazzy new design element.

What You Need

X **Basic Sewing Kit (page 11)**

X **Basic Pattern**

X **Fabric (Refer to the chart at right)**

X **Large piece of paper**

X **1 button**

X **Pencil**

X **Ruler or measuring tape**

Seam allowances:
  ⅝ **inch (1.6 cm) unless otherwise noted**

Shown in size 8

What You Do

Alter the Pattern

1 Make note of the triple notches on the back pattern piece. Alter the pattern on a large piece of paper. Draw a straight line across the dress back pattern piece through the middle of the triple notch. Measure the distance from the bottom of the armhole to the drawn line along the side seam. Mark that measurement on the dress front pattern piece side seam and draw a straight line across the front, starting at the side seam marking (figure 1).

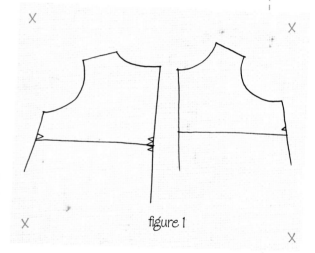

figure 1

	SIZE 3	SIZE 4	SIZE 5	SIZE 6	SIZE 7	SIZE 8
SOLID FABRIC (BODICE AND FACINGS)	¾ yd (68.6 cm)	1 yd (0.9 m)	1 yd (0.9 m)	1¼ yd (1.1 m)	1½ yd (1.4 m)	1½ yd (1.4 m)
PLAID FABRIC (SKIRT)	½ yd (45.7 cm)	½ yd (45.7 cm)	1 yd (0.9 m)	1 yd (0.9 m)	1¼ yd (1.1 m)	1½ yd (1.4 m)
Yardage is the same for all fabric widths.						

2 Cut the newly drawn lines on both the front and the back pattern pieces. Add ¼ inch (6 mm) to the bottom of the top pieces and ¼ inch (6 mm) to the top of the bottom pieces for seam allowance.

Make the Dress

1 Cut the top pieces and facings from the solid fabric. Cut the bottom dress front and back pieces on the bias grainline (page 16) from the plaid fabric.

2 Sew the front top piece to the front bottom piece with the right sides together and ¼-inch (6 mm) seam allowance. Press the seam open. Repeat with the back top and bottom pieces.

3 Continue making the dress according to the basic instructions (page 30), steps 2 through 16. Pop this on over a turtleneck and your girl's ready for the first day of school.

Note

While this dress looks lovely in wool plaid, you could make a pretty warm-weather version using lightweight fabrics.

Designer Joan K. Morris

Candy Stripes

This dress is yummy eye candy! It features fancy piecing created with a playful mix of fabric panels.

What You Need

X **Basic Sewing Kit (page 11)**

X **Basic Pattern**

X **Fabric (Refer to the chart at right)**

X **1 button**

Seam allowances:

⅝ inch (1.6 cm) unless otherwise noted

Shown in size 4

What You Do

Cut and Prepare the Fabric

1 Make two squares of pieced fabric large enough to accommodate the pattern pieces in the size you wish to make. For example, for this size 4 dress, the panels were cut 25 inches (63.5 cm) long and to the following widths: floral fabric, 5 inches (12.7 cm); pink fabric and yellow fabric, 4 inches (10.2 cm); and striped fabric, 6 inches (15.2 cm). Adjust the widths as needed.

2 Arrange the fabric strips as shown, with the stripes running horizontally (figure 1).

3 Sew the strips with the right sides together and ½-inch (1.3 cm) seam allowances. Press the seams toward the darker fabric. When you're finished, you'll have a rectangle of pieced fabric large enough to accommodate the pattern.

4 Repeat step 3 with the remaining fabric strips, making a matching rectangle of fabric.

5 Cut out the facings from the solid pink fabric.

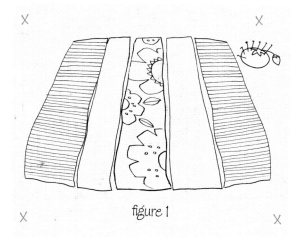

figure 1

	SIZE 3	SIZE 4	SIZE 5	SIZE 6	SIZE 7	SIZE 8
FLORAL COTTON	⅓ yd (30.5 cm)	⅓ yd (30.5 cm)	⅓ yd (30.5 cm)	⅓ yd (30.5 cm)	⅓ yd (30.5 cm)	⅓ yd (30.5 cm)
PINK COTTON	½ yd (45.7 cm)	¾ yd (68.6 m)	¾ yd (68.6 m)	¾ yd (68.6 m)	1 yd (0.9 m)	1 yd (0.9 m)
YELLOW COTTON	¼ yd (22.9 cm)	¼ yd (22.9 cm)	¼ yd (22.9 cm)	¼ yd (22.9 cm)	¼ yd (22.9 cm)	¼ yd (22.9 cm)
PINK COTTON	1 yd (0.9 m)	1 yd (0.9 m)	1 yd (0.9 m)	1 yd (0.9 m)	1 yd (0.9 m)	1 yd (0.9 m)

Yardage is the same for all fabric widths.

Make the Dress

1 Fold each of the pieced rectangles in half lengthwise along the center of the floral fabric. Pin the front pattern piece along the fold of one piece and cut out the front piece. Pin the back pattern piece parallel to the fold and cut out the back piece (figure 2).

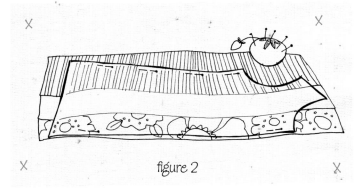

figure 2

2 Follow the basic pattern instructions (page 30), step 2 through step 16 to finish the dress.

Tip
Make sure all your fabrics are of similar weights.

Here's a dress for Daddy's little sweetheart—the piping is made from old ties to add pattern and panache to this colorful version of the A-line.

What You Need

X **Basic Sewing Kit (page 11)**

X **Basic Pattern**

X **Fabric (Refer to the chart at right)**

X **6 or more ties**

X **5 yards (4.6 m) of ³/₁₆-inch (4.8 mm) cotton cording**

X **3 covered button sets, ³/₄ inch (1.9 cm) in diameter**

X **1 hook-and-eye closure**

X **Zipper presser foot**

X **Hand-sewing needle and thread**

Seam allowances:

⅝ inch (1.6 cm) unless otherwise noted

Shown in size 6

All Tied Up

What You Do

Cut the Fabric

The following measurements are for a size 6 dress. Measure the size of the pattern you are going to make, and increase or decrease the size of the rectangles accordingly.

1 From the purple fabric, cut two 10½ x 24-inch (26.7 x 61 cm) pieces and two 2½ x 6¼-inch (6.4 x 15.9 cm) pieces. Save the rest of the fabric for the facings.

2 From both the blue and the green fabrics, cut two 10½ x 24-inch (26.7 x 61 cm) pieces.

Make the Piping

1 Open up the ties using scissors and a seam ripper. Remove the inside facings and throw them away. Press the ties flat. (Most ties are silk, so use a low setting on the iron.)

2 Cut the ties into as many 2 x 8-inch (5.1 x 20.3 cm) rectangles as possible.

3 Join the tie strips at the short ends, alternating colors and patterns. To join the strips without adding too much bulk, place the ends at a 90° angle and machine stitch from corner to corner so the seam is at an angle (figure 1). Trim the seam allowance, which is a triangle of extra fabric. Repeat until you have 5 yards (4.6 m) of joined ties.

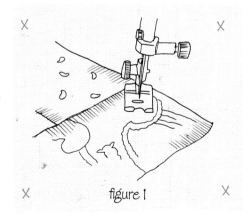

figure 1

	SIZE 3	SIZE 4	SIZE 5	SIZE 6	SIZE 7	SIZE 8
PURPLE FABRIC	½ yd (45.7 cm)	¾ yd (68.6 m)	¾ yd (68.6 m)	¾ yd (68.6 m)	1 yd (0.9 m)	1 yd (0.9 m)
GREEN AND BLUE FABRICS	1¼ yd (22.9 cm)	⅓ yd (30.5 cm)	⅓ yd (30.5 m)	½ yd (45.7 m)	½ yd (45.7 m)	½ yd (45.7 m)

Yardage is th___ ___ fabric widths.

4 Install a zipper presser foot on your sewing machine. Place the cotton cording in the middle of the tie strip, with the wrong side of the tie strip facing up. Fold the tie strip around the cording and stitch as close as possible to the cording (figure 2). Leave the zipper presser foot on the machine.

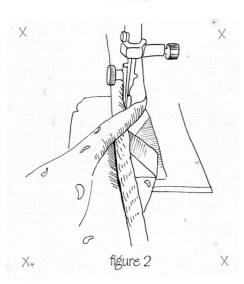

figure 2

5 Trim the raw edges of the tie strip to ⅝ inch (1.6 cm) from the cord. Congratulations! You just made custom piping!

Designer Joan K. Morris

Attach the Piping

1 Cut four pieces of the piping each as long as the longest measurement of the fabric rectangles cut in the Cut the Fabric section on page 108.

2 Lay out one set of the cut rectangles with the purple at the top, green in the middle, and blue at the bottom. Place a piece of piping on the right side of the bottom edge of the purple fabric with the raw edges aligned. Baste the piping to the fabric as close as possible to the cord.

3 Pin the green and purple fabrics with right sides together and the piping sandwiched between them. Stitch all three layers together as close to the cord as possible.

4 Place a piece of piping on the right side of the bottom edge of the green fabric with the raw edges aligned. Baste the piping to the fabric as close as possible to the cord. Repeat step 3 to join the blue fabric to the green.

5 With the remaining pieces of fabric, repeat steps 2 through 4 to make a second panel of joined fabrics.

Tip
Choose fabrics of similar weights for this project.

Cut the Fabric

1 Fold each of the panels in half with the piping running horizontally. Make sure the piping is aligned. Pin the front pattern piece to one of the panels with the center front line on the fabric fold and the top of the pattern on the purple fabric. Make marks on the side seam of the pattern at the piping locations. Cut the front fabric.

2 Place the front and back pattern pieces together at the side seams and copy the piping location marks from the front pattern piece onto the back pattern piece, so you can line up the piping at the side seams.

3 Pin the back pattern piece onto the other fabric panel, so that the marks on the side seam line up with the piping on the fabric; the center back should run parallel to the fold. Cut two back pieces.

4 Cut the facings from extra purple fabric.

Make the Dress

1 Staystitch (page 18) the curved front and back neck edges, ½ inch (1.3 cm) from the cut edge, and stitch the shoulder seams together as in the basic instructions (page 30).

2 Cut pieces of piping the length of the neck and armholes. Place a piece of piping at the neck, aligning the raw edges. Baste close to the cord, easing the stitching around the curves. Repeat for both armholes.

3 Follow the basic instructions on page 30, beginning with step 4, to finish making the dress. Use the zipper foot when joining the facings to the dress at the neck and armholes.

4 To make the faux placket, baste a length of piping around two short and one long edge of one of the small purple pieces of fabric. With right sides together, pin the remaining purple piece to the piped piece. Stitch through all three layers around all sides, leaving a 2-inch (5.1 cm) opening on the side without piping. Clip the corners and turn the piece right side out. Use the point turner to neaten the corners. Tuck the raw edges of the opening to the inside, hand stitch the opening closed (page 19), and press the piece.

5 Position the placket on the center front of the dress, and machine stitch it in place on three edges, leaving the long edge with the piping unstitched.

6 Following the manufacturer's instructions, cover the three buttons with leftover tie fabric and stitch them onto the placket.

Add a kicky pleated skirt to your dress for an updated schoolgirl style. This look can work as a jumper, too.

What You Need

X **Basic Sewing Kit (page 11)**

X **Basic Pattern**

X **Fabric (Refer to the chart at right)**

X **½ yard (45.7 cm) of cotton fabric for the sash**

X **Large piece of paper**

X **1 hook-and-eye closure**

X **Pencil**

X **Ruler**

X **Hand-sewing needle and thread**

X **Safety pin**

Seam allowances:
⅝ inch (1.6 cm) unless otherwise noted

Shown in size 4

Too Cool for School

What You Do

Alter the Pattern

1 Hold the front dress pattern up to your child and mark the hipline or the desired location of the contrast band. Draw a straight line across the pattern at the desired location. Either trace the pattern above the line onto new paper to save the basic pattern, or cut off the bottom part of the pattern. Measure and make note of the length of the bottom of the pattern below the line (for the new pleated piece). Subtract 2½ inches (6.4 cm) from this measurement for the width of the sash; you'll use this measurement to cut the new, pleated bottom of the dress (see Cut the Fabric). You can discard the bottom of the pattern. The top is the new dress front pattern piece.

2 Align the side seam of the new front pattern piece with the back pattern piece and mark the position of the line on the back pattern piece. Draw the same line and trace the new dress back or cut off the bottom of the pattern piece. The top is the new dress back pattern piece.

Cut the Fabric

1 Cut one dress front (on the fabric fold), two dress backs, and the facings from the dress fabric. For the pleated skirt, cut two pieces that are each the length measurement as determined in step 1 by the width referenced in the chart below.

PLEATING CHART Pleat width 2¾ inches (7 cm); pleat depth 1⅜ inches (3.5 cm)		
SIZE	FIRST PLEAT LOCATION	FABRIC WIDTH
3	2½ inches (6.4 cm)	43½ inches (110.5 cm)
4	2¾ inches (7 cm)	44 inches (111.8 cm)
5	3 inches (7.6 cm)	44½ inches (113 cm)
6	3¼ inches (8.3 cm)	45 inches (114.3 cm)
7	3½ inches (8.9 cm)	45½ inches (115.6 cm)
8	3¾ inches (9.5 cm)	46 inches (116.8 cm)

	SIZE 3	SIZE 4	SIZE 5	SIZE 6	SIZE 7	SIZE 8
MAIN FABRIC	2¼ yd (2 m)	2¼ yd (2 m)	2½ yd (2.3 m)	2¾ yd (2.5 m)	2¾ yd (2.5 m)	3 yd (2.7 m)
Yardage is the same for all fabric widths.						

2 From the sash fabric, cut four pieces that are 3¾ inches (9.5 cm) by the bottom width of your dress. Two of these pieces will be the sash, and two will be the sash lining.

Make the Dress

1. Hem the bottom of the skirt pieces by pressing ¼ inch (6 mm) to the wrong side. Press another 1¼ inches (3.2 cm) to the wrong side and edgestitch as close to the folded edge as possible.

2 Place one of the hemmed skirt pieces on the ironing board, wrong side up. Refer to the Pleating Chart and reference your size for the following: working from one short end, measure in the amount listed as First Pleat Location and press a fold to the left at this spot. Measure 1⅜ inches (3.5 cm) from the first fold and press a second fold line back to the right. Keep folding the rectangle back and forth, alternating between 2¾ inches (7 cm) and 1⅜ inches (3.5 cm) until the entire skirt is pleated; also alternate folding to the left and right as shown (figure 1). Baste across the top edge to hold the folds in place.

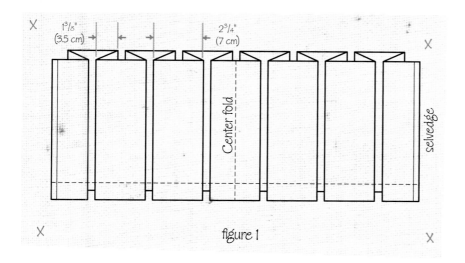

1³⁄₈" (3.5 cm)   2³⁄₄" (7 cm)

Center fold

selvedge

figure 1

3 Pin one of the sash pieces to the top edge of the pleated skirt with the right sides together. Stitch with a ½-inch (1.3 cm) seam allowance. Press the seam toward the sash.

4 Repeat steps 2 and 3 with the other hemmed skirt piece.

5 The skirt/sash, dress front, and sash lining will all be stitched together at the same time. Make a sandwich as follows, aligning the raw edges: skirt/sash, right side up; bottom of dress front, wrong side up; sash lining, wrong side up (figure 2).

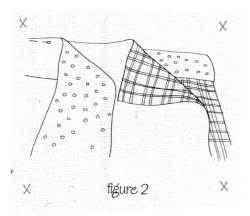

figure 2

6 Stitch all three layers together with a ½-inch (1.3 cm) seam allowance. Press all the pieces toward the sash.

7 Press the loose edge of the sash lining ½ inch (1.3 cm) to the wrong side and slipstitch the folded edge to cover the seam inside the dress.

8 Stitch the center back seam of the top back pieces with the right sides together, up about 3 inches (7.6 cm) from the bottom edge. Press the seam open.

9 Attach the remaining pleated skirt/sash to the top back as in steps 5 through 7.

10 Follow the basic instructions on page 30 from steps 2 through 15 to finish sewing the dress. Sew the hook and eye at the back neck closing.

Make the Bow

1 Cut a piece of the sash fabric 2½ x 19 inches (5.1 x 48.3 cm). Fold the piece in half with the right sides together so the short ends meet. Stitch both long edges together with a ½-inch (1.3 cm) seam allowance. Turn it right side out and press it flat.

2 Measure 5 inches (12.7 cm) from the short, folded edge and cut the piece in two.

3 Fold the ends of the longer piece into the middle, overlapping them by ½ inch (1.3 cm). Machine stitch across the overlapping ends. Pinch the center of the bow together and hand stitch the gathers.

4 Wrap the remaining piece around the gathered center so the finished end overlaps the unfinished end. Hand sew this piece in place. Be sure to catch some of the bow in the stitching so the center knot can't slide off the bow.

5 Slip a safety pin through the wrong side of the center of the bow and pin it to the sash. Always remember to remove the bow before washing the dress.

Wearing this charming A-line dress will make your little girl feel like she is wandering through a garden. Bands of colorful fabrics and appliquéd poppies are sure to bring a smile to the wearer—and everyone who sees her.

What You Need

- X Basic Sewing Kit (page 11)
- X Basic Pattern
- X Pocket and Poppies Templates (page 128)
- X Fabric (Refer to the chart on page 118)
- X Cotton remnants in green, black, light, and dark red
- X Large piece of paper, twice the size as the pattern front
- X Gold and red thread
- X 2 black, four-hole buttons, ⅝ inch (1.6 cm) diameter
- X Pencil
- X Ruler or yardstick
- X Hand-sewing needle

Seam allowances:
⅝ inch (1.6 cm) unless otherwise noted

Shown in size 4

Poppies Afield

What You Do

Alter the Pattern

1 Trace the pattern front and back onto paper, so you don't mark up the basic A-line pattern pieces, in case you want to make more dresses.

2 To change the curved neckline to a square neckline, measure and mark 1 inch (2.5 cm) down from the top of the center front line. Draw a new cutting line straight across the pattern from the marking to the armhole and cut the pattern directly on the line. Discard the pattern piece above the cut line (figure 1).

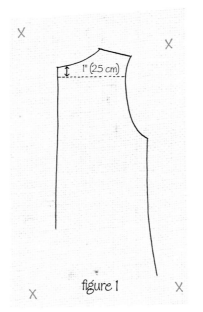

figure 1

3 Trace the new dress front piece to make a dress front lining pattern. From the tracing, cut 1 inch (2.5 cm) up from the hem to make the lining shorter than the dress.

4 On the dress front pattern, draw three design lines parallel to the top edge of the dress. The first line should be 3 inches (7.6 cm) below the top edge, the second 1¾ inches (4.4 cm) below the first line, and the last line 1½ inches (3.8 cm) below the second line. Before you cut the dress front pattern apart and add seam allowances to these pieces, use it as a guide to cut the dress back. Mark the top strip medium blue, the middle strip light blue, and the bottom strip green (figure 2).

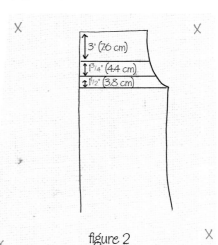

figure 2

Designer Shannon Udell

5 Trace the dress back pattern piece onto clean paper, removing the ⅝-inch (1.6 cm) seam allowance from the center back seam. Make a note to cut the dress back with the center back of the pattern piece along the fold of the fabric. Draw extended shoulders between 5 and 8 inches (12.7 and 20.3 cm) long, depending on the size of the child, to make straps that go over the shoulders and reach the dress front. You might want to hold the pattern up to your child to make sure the extended shoulders are long enough. Round the ends (figure 3).

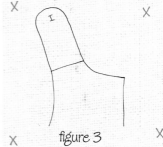

figure 3

6 Trace the new dress back pattern piece with the extended shoulders to make a dress back lining pattern. From the tracing, cut 1 inch (2.5 cm) up from the hem.

	SIZE 3	SIZE 4	SIZE 5	SIZE 6	SIZE 7	SIZE 8
MEDIUM BLUE FABRIC (TOP STRIPE AND LINING)	1 yd (0.9 m)	1¼ yd (1.1 m)	1¼ yd (1.1 m)	1¼ yd (1.1 m)	1¼ yd (1.1 m)	1¼ yd (1.1 m)
LIGHT BLUE AND GREEN FABRICS (DRESS STRIPES)	⅛ yd (11.4 cm)	⅛ yd (11.4 cm)	⅛ yd (11.4 cm)	⅛ yd (11.4 cm)	⅛ yd (11.4 cm)	⅛ yd (11.4 cm)
GREEN POLKA-DOT FABRIC (SKIRT)	1 yd (0.9 m)	1 yd (0.9 m)	1 yd (0.9 m)	1¼ yd (1.1 m)	1¼ yd (1.1 m)	1¼ yd (1.1 m)

Yardage is the same for all fabric widths.

7 Lay the new, marked dress front pattern piece on the dress back pattern piece, and starting from the hem edge mark the same cutting lines across the back. The top piece of the dress back will be considerably longer than the top piece of the dress front because of the different necklines; however, they should be the same length at the side seam.

8 Cut on the marked lines. Trace all the pieces onto clean paper, adding ⅝-inch (1.6 cm) seam allowances to the top and bottom of all the cut edges, except only add seam allowance to the lower edges of the very top pieces and to the upper edges of the lower/skirt pieces. These are your new dress front and back pattern pieces.

Cut the Fabric

1 From the medium blue fabric, cut: one front lining, one back lining, one top dress front, and one top dress back with the center front and back of all the patterns placed on the fabric fold.

2 From the light blue fabric, cut: the middle pieces for the dress front and back with the center front and back of the patterns along the fabric fold.

3 From the light green fabric, cut: the bottom strips for the dress front and back with the center front and back of the patterns along the fabric fold. Cut one pocket, using the template on page 128.

4 From the green polka-dot fabric, cut: the skirt pieces for the dress front and back with the center front and back of the patterns along the fabric fold.

Piece the Dress

1 Refer to the photograph to piece the dress front and back. Sew all the seams with the right sides of the fabric together and ⅝-inch (1.6 cm) seam allowances, and press the seams toward the hem of the dress.

2 Sew the medium blue pieces to the light blue pieces. Sew the light green pieces to the light blue pieces. Finally, sew the polka-dot green skirt pieces to the light green pieces.

3 Press ½ inch (1.3 cm) to the wrong side on the curved bottom edge of the pocket. Press the top of the pocket ¼ inch (6 mm) and then 1¼ inches (3.2 cm) to the wrong side and stitch close to the inside folded edge.

4 Refer to the photograph, or choose any location, and edgestitch (page 18) the pocket in place on the dress front.

Embellish the Dress

1 Enlarge the templates on page 128 and use them to cut a variety of different size green stems, large dark red poppy shapes, small light red poppy insides, and black centers.

2 Lay out and pin a variety of different length stems on the front and back bodice, and under the top edge of the pocket, so ¼ inch (6 mm) of the bottom of each stem overlaps the color strip it will seem to grow out of (or is under the pocket). Fold the extra ¼ inch (6 mm) under and hand stitch the folded edges in place. Topstitch (page 18) the edges of the stems in place using gold thread. Stitch around each shape two times for a more dramatic, crafty effect. Be sure to position two front stems so they reach to the top corner of the dress, so the poppies on each strap will appear to be atop the stems.

3 Arrange the poppies with the darker red on bottom, lighter red in the middle, and black on top. Save two large poppies (without the center black circles) for the shoulder extensions. Pin or baste the poppy layers together. Thread your sewing machine with gold thread in the needle and machine stitch the layers in a random circle inside the black circles.

4 Thread your sewing machine with red thread and straight machine stitch the poppies onto the dress, at the top of each stem (except for the two poppies that go on the shoulder strap extensions). Stitch around the edge of each piece three times.

5 When the front and back appliqués (except on the straps) are sewn on, clip stray threads, but expect a homespun, frayed look.

Finish the Dress

1 Sew the dress front to the back at the sides with right sides together. Be sure to match the piecing seams. Press the seams to the back. Repeat with the lining front and back.

2 Pin the dress to the lining at the armhole and neck with the right sides together. Starting at one of the side seams, sew all the way around the top of the dress. Clip all the curves, turn the dress right side out, and press.

3 Pin two large red poppies, with the smaller red poppy pieces (without the black centers), to the ends of the shoulder straps and stitch them in place. For added strength in such a high-use area, circle each piece between five and seven times (figure 4).

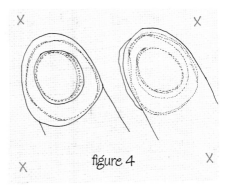

figure 4

4 Stitch a vertical buttonhole (page 28) long enough to accommodate a ⅝-inch (1.6 cm) button in the center of each flower, using red thread.

5 Sew a black button to each corner stem on the front dress using gold thread in an X pattern.

6 Hem the dress and lining separately by pressing the bottom ½ inch (1.3 cm) and then ½ inch (1.3 cm) again to the wrong side and machine stitch along the fold. The lining should be about 1 inch (2.5 cm) shorter than the dress. You're done. Pat yourself on the back and wait for the compliments to roll in.

Make a Hair Accessory
Can't get enough poppies? Make a hair accessory to match your lovely dress!

What You Need

X 1 x 10 inch (2.5 x 25.4 cm) rectangle of dark red fabric

X Circle of light red fabric, 1¾ inches (4.5 cm) in diameter

X Circle of dark green felt, 1½ inches (3.8 cm) in diameter

X Gold and red thread

X 1 black button

X 1 hair clip, bobby pin, scrunchie, or fabric headband

X Pinking shears

X Hand-sewing needle

1 Cut one long side of the dark red fabric and around the light red circle with pinking shears.

2 Press the straight edge and one short side of the dark red fabric ¼ inch (6 mm) to the wrong side. Hand baste along the long, folded edge with the gold thread and pull the thread to make a gathered, but flat, circle. Make sure the folded short end is overlapping the right side of the poppy. Stitch a knot to hold the flower tight, trim the thread, and press flat.

3 Pin the felt circle to the wrong side of the large gathered circle and machine stitch, with the red thread, a circle ½ inch (1.3 cm) in diameter in the center to keep the pieces together.

4 Pin the smaller red circle to the right side of the top of the gathered circle and machine stitch a circle ¾ inch (1.9 cm) three times in the center of the poppy, again with red thread.

5 With the gold thread, stitch the button to the center of the poppy in an X pattern. Pull the thread through to the back and make a knot. Use the same thread to attach the poppy to a hair clip, bobby pin, scrunchie, or fabric headband.

Designer Valerie Shrader

Vibrant shades of silk dupioni transform this bubble-hem dress. Add a hand-dyed silk ribbon at the waist and your princess is ready for any party. How can something so simple look so spectacular?

What You Need

X Basic Sewing Kit (page 11)

X Basic Pattern

X Fabric (Refer to the chart on page 124)

X Large piece of paper

X 1 button, ½ inch (1.3 cm) in diameter

X 2 yards (1.8 m) of silk ribbon, 1½ inches (3.8 cm) wide

X Pencil

X Clear ruler

X Dressmaker's curve

X Dressmaker's chalk or disappearing-ink pen

Seam allowances:
    ⅝ inch (1.6 cm) unless otherwise noted

Shown in size 7

Bubble Skirt

What You Do

Alter the Pattern

1 Trace the pattern front and back onto paper, so you don't mark up the basic A-line pattern pieces, in case you want to make more dresses.

2 Draw a straight line across the front and back pattern pieces to divide them into a skirt and bodice, using the clear ruler and the waistline markings on the pattern as a guide. Make sure the line is the same distance below the armhole at the side seam on both pieces (figure 1). Cut along the marked lines. Add a ⅝-inch (1.6 cm) seam allowance to the bottom of the bodice and to the top of the skirt.

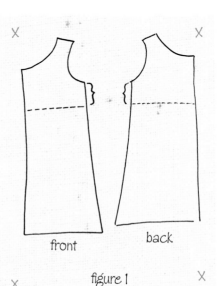

front   back

figure 1

3 To make the front and back skirt lining pattern pieces, trace a front and back skirt that is ½ to 1 inch (1.3 to 2.5 cm) shorter than the existing skirt patterns.

4 Alter the hem edge of the skirt pattern pieces as follows: measure out from the bottom edge at the side seam 6 inches (15.2 cm), using the dressmaker's curve to retain the curve of the skirt, and mark. This will add a total of 24 inches (61 cm) to the hem circumference of the skirt; for the smaller sizes, you may wish to add less width. Draw new side seams on both pieces, using the straight ruler to connect the waist to the marking.

Cut the Fabric

1 Cut the bodice front, bodice back, and facing pieces from silk B and set them aside.

2 Cut the skirt front and back lining pieces from muslin. Starting at one side seam, make four evenly spaced markings along the lower edge of each piece. You'll use these to match the fabric skirt to the lining.

3 Cut the bubble skirt from the altered pattern pieces and silk A. Starting at one side seam, make four evenly spaced markings along the lower edge of each piece. You'll use these to match the fabric skirt to the lining.

Make the Dress

1 Construct the bodice as in the basic dress instructions, page 30, following steps 2 through 8.

2 Stitch the skirt lining center back seam with the right sides of the fabric together. Stitch the skirt front lining to the skirt back lining at the side seams with the right sides together. Repeat with the skirt fabric pieces.

3 Sew two rows of gathering stitches around the lower edge of the fabric skirt, beginning and ending at each side seam. You don't want one long continuous set of stitches; instead, gather the front and back separately.

4 Pull the stitches to gather the bottom edge of the skirt. With the right sides together, pin the fabric bottom to the lining bottom, matching the side seams and the marks on the skirt and lining. Adjust the gathers as necessary, and stitch the seam. Trim the seam allowances and turn the skirt right side out.

5 Pin and baste the top edge of the lining to the top edge of the skirt with the wrong sides together. Pin the skirt to the bodice with right sides together, matching the side and center back seams, and stitch.

6 Sew the button to the upper right side of the bodice, and make a wrapped thread loop on the left side (page 28). Make wrapped thread loops at the waistline to keep the ribbon belt in place. Thread the ribbon through the loops. Hey, little Cinderella, listen out for the stroke of midnight!

	SIZE 3	SIZE 4	SIZE 5	SIZE 6	SIZE 7	SIZE 8
SILK A (SKIRT)	1 yd (0.9 m)	1 yd (0.9 m)	1 yd (0.9 m)	1¼ yd (1.1 m)	1¼ yd (1.1 m)	1½ yd (1.4 m)
SILK B (BODICE AND FACINGS)	¾ yd (68.6 cm)	¾ yd (68.6 cm)	1 yd (0.9 m)	1 yd (0.9 m)	1 yd (0.9 m)	1 yd (0.9 m)
MUSLIN LINING	½ yd (45.7 cm)	½ yd (45.7 cm)	1 yd (0.9 m)	1¼ yd (1.1 m)	1¼ yd (1.1 m)	1½ yd (1.4 m)
Yardage is the same for all fabric widths.						

Templates

Puttin' on the Ritz
page 86

enlarge 200%

8
7
6
5
4
3

Floral Arrangements,
page 34

enlarge 200%

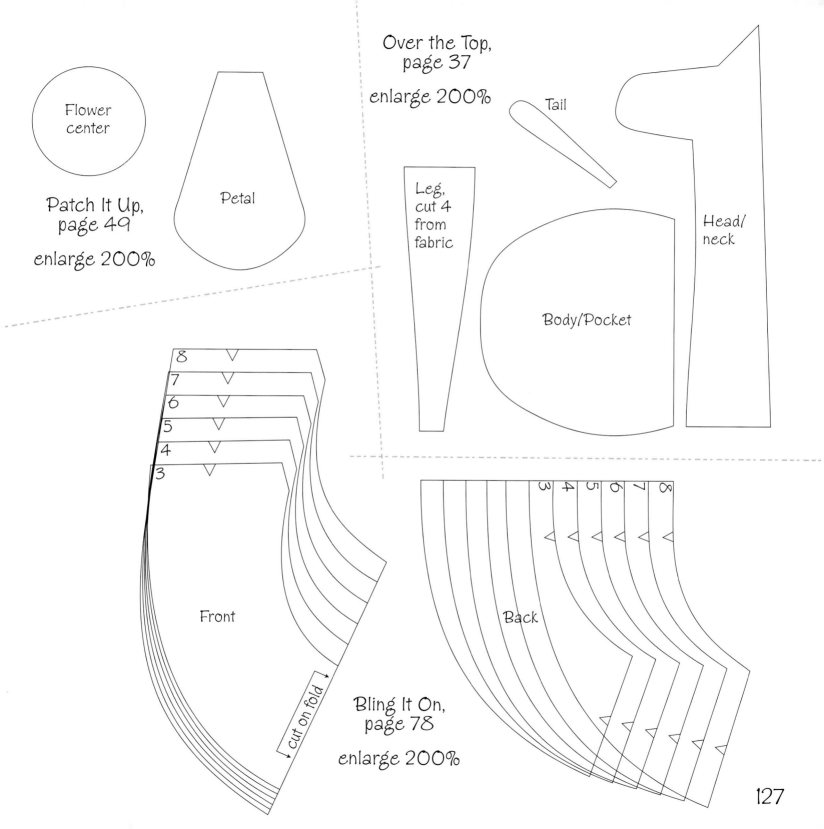

Flower
center

Patch It Up,
page 49

enlarge 200%

Petal

Over the Top,
page 37

enlarge 200%

Tail

Leg,
cut 4
from
fabric

Body/Pocket

Head/
neck

8
7
6
5
4
3

Front

cut on fold

Bling It On,
page 78

enlarge 200%

3
4
5
6
7
8

Back

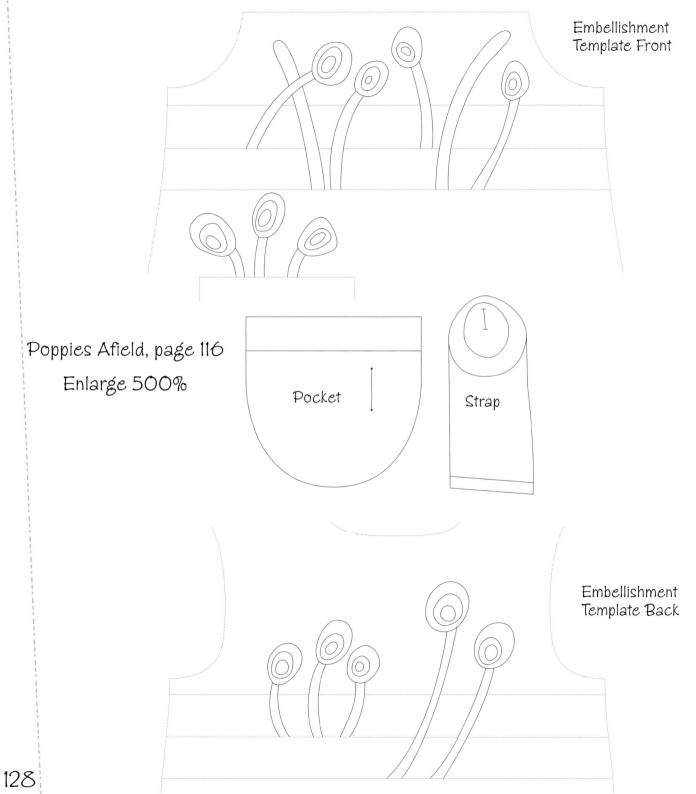

Embellishment
Template Front

Poppies Afield, page 116

Enlarge 500%

Pocket

Strap

Embellishment
Template Back

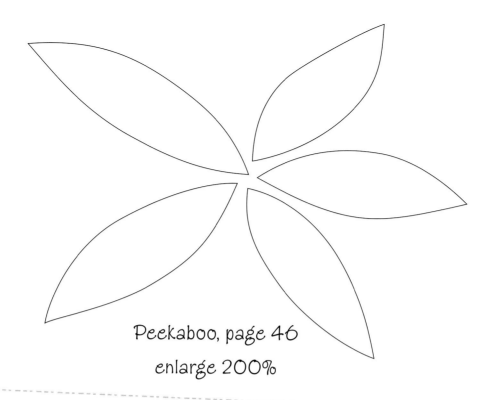

Peekaboo, page 46

enlarge 200%

Enchanted Woodland, page 43

enlarge 200%

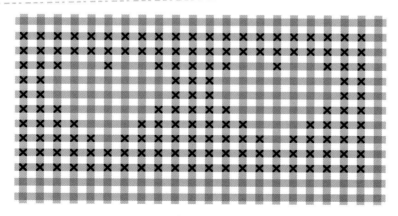

Cross My Heart, page 41

enlarge 200%

About the Designers

Betsy Couzins has worked as a mixed-media artist since the second grade, when she received an "A" for her pilgrim diorama. Her work has been featured in the Lark books *A Is for Apron* (2008), *Pretty Little Potholders* (2008), *Altered Art* (2004), and *The Decorated Journal* (2006), as well as several national periodicals, including *Jane* and *Artitude*. Betsy currently resides in Asheville, North Carolina, with her husband and son. She chronicles her increasing love of working with fabric on her blog at www.wonderland5.typepad.com.

Rebeka Lambert is a self-proclaimed fabric addict living on the outskirts of Baton Rouge, Louisiana, with her husband and three young children. Her love of sewing began as a child when she would watch her mother and grandmother sew, but it was the discovery of craft blogs that led her back to crafting. She has contributed to Lark books including *Pretty Little Patchwork* (2008) and *Pretty Little Purses and Pouches* (2008). You can catch a glimpse of Rebeka's life on her blog, www.artsycraftybabe.typepad.com, or at her Etsy shop, www.artsycraftybabe.etsy.com, where she periodically sells her creations.

Joan K. Morris's artistic endeavors have led her down many successful creative paths, including costume design for motion pictures and ceramics. Joan has contributed projects for numerous Lark books, including *Extreme Office Crafts* (2007), *Cutting-Edge Decoupage* (2007), *Pretty Little Pincushions* (2007), *Button! Button!* (2008), *Pretty Little Potholders* (2008), *50 Nifty Beaded Cards* (2008), and many, many other titles.

Aimee Ray has been making things for as long as she can remember. Between working as a graphic designer in the greeting card and comic book industries and balancing her own personal projects, she's almost never without something creative in hand. Her interests span from digital painting and illustration to sewing stuffed animals and embroidery. She is the author of *Doodle Stitching* (Lark Books, 2007), a book of contemporary embroidery designs and projects. You can see more of Aimee's work at her website, www.dreamfollow.com.

Old memories inspire many of **Dorie Blaisdell Schwarz's** designs, whether they're created on a sewing machine, with knitting needles, as a screen print, or with a hot-glue gun in hand. She currently lives in Farmer City, Illinois, with her husband and their young daughter. When she's not sewing or crafting, she's building websites and renovating her Victorian-era farmhouse. Pay her a visit at tumblingblocks.net.

Valerie Shrader made a pair of pink culottes when she was 11 and has loved fabric (and sewing) ever since. She's a senior editor at Lark Books and has written and edited many books related to textiles and needlework. Valerie knits every now and then, too, and dreams about dyeing fabric and making artful quilts when she's not watching birds.

Shannon Udell designs funky little fabric patches, dolls, art quilts, and other goodies from her residence in California. She shares this creative home with her husband, Scott, crafty daughters, Megan and Brigit, and their two lazy dogs. When she's not sewing, she's in her garden or reading a great book.

About the Author

Wendi Gratz lives down the road from the Penland School of Crafts in western North Carolina with her family and sewing machine. In high school, she chose to skip home economics in favor of wood and metal shop classes, so she didn't learn how to use a sewing machine until college! Her first project, a disastrous attempt at a tablecloth, taught her a lot, so her second project—designing and making all the costumes for a play—was more successful. Now she makes fun clothes, funky dolls, and all kinds of quilts. You can see her work at www.wendigratz.com.

Acknowledgments

This book couldn't have come together without the talents and support of a whole lot of people.

A huge thank you to the project designers who contributed their considerable sewing flair. I'm grateful to my editor, Valerie Van Arsdale Shrader, and to the editorial team at Lark Books that tied up (and snipped off) all the loose threads: intern Jacob Biba, Kathleen Mc-Cafferty, Nathalie Mornu, and Gavin Young. Let's not forget Susan McBride and her sweet illustrations, or Carol Morse for her attention to detail during art production.

Photographer Steve Mann took fantastic pictures under the art direction of Megan Kirby. Give it up for those adorable little girls who modeled for them: Cassidy and Deja Burry, Angelina Dumigron, Eva and Mayla Hetzel, Holt and Ryland Mettee, Margaret Murphy, Ellery Parmenter, Kayla Schmidt, Amara Steiner, Emily Stokes, Aislin Thompson, Meghan and Helen Vance, and Lucy Wrenn.

Thanks to my mom and dad, Bob and Carol Winters, for raising me in a house full of craft supplies and the spirit of experimentation. I'm forever indebted to my mother-in-law, Dot Gratz, for my fabulous sewing machine, which I use every day.

Finally, thanks to my husband, Alan—for everything.

Index

It's all on www.larkbooks.com

Can't find the materials you
need to create a project?
Search our database for craft suppliers
& sources for hard-to-find materials.

Got an idea for a book?
Read our book proposal
guidelines and contact us.

Want to show off your work?
Browse current calls for entries.

Want to know what new and
exciting books we're working on?
Sign up for our free e-newsletter.

Feeling crafty?
Find free, downloadable
project directions on the site.

Interested in learning more about
the authors, designers & editors
who create Lark books?